PRAYER
YOUR
FOUNDATION
FOR
SUCCESS

KENNETH COPELAND

KENNETH
COPELAND
PUBLICATIONS

Prayer—Your Foundation for Success

ISBN-10 0-88114-704-4   30-0019
ISBN-13 978-0-88114-704-9

21 20 19 18 17 16   34 33 32 31 30 29

© 1983 Kenneth Copeland

Kenneth Copeland Publications
Fort Worth, TX 76192-0001

For more information about Kenneth Copeland Ministries, visit kcm.org or call 1-800-600-7395 (U.S. only) or +1-817-852-6000.

Contents

A Message From Kenneth Copeland

Early in my ministry, I learned a vital lesson: For any effort to be successful, it must be backed by prayer. Effective praying is the key to success in every area of life.

Your aim in prayer is to be effective. Jesus is the perfect example of One who knows how to pray and get results. He spent hours separated from the people, praying and fellowshiping with His heavenly Father. The time He spent in prayer prepared Him to minister effectively.

As a believer, you can achieve the same results Jesus did during His earthly ministry—and more. Jesus said, "He that believeth on me, the works that I do shall he do also; and greater works than these shall he do; because I go unto my Father" (John 14:12). These "greater works" can be accomplished today, but only by believers who have a deep, sincere prayer life with God.

This book is designed to strengthen your relationship with God through an awareness of the importance of prayer. With a solid foundation from the Word of God, you will understand the basic principles of prayer: its purpose, how to pray and how to get results.

As you read and study *Prayer—Your Foundation for Success,* I pray, according to Ephesians 1:17-18, that you will have the spirit of wisdom and revelation in the knowledge of God and that the eyes of your understanding will be enlightened to know the truth.

—Kenneth Copeland

Chapter 1
Prayer Secrets

Prayer is the foundation of every successful Christian endeavor. Time spent with God is vital if you desire a fruitful Christian life. As the foundation of every Christian endeavor, it plays a vital role in living a successful Christian life. Study the lives of the great men and women of God from the past, and you'll see the strong emphasis they placed on prayer. Without prayer, they would never have been able to achieve such tremendous results.

Throughout the New Testament we can see the value of prayer in the founding of the early churches. The Apostle Paul prayed and interceded many hours for the new believers. In Ephesians 1:16 he wrote, "[I] Cease not to give thanks for you, making mention of you in my prayers." In Colossians 1:3 he said, "We give thanks to God and the Father of our Lord Jesus Christ, praying always for you." In 1 Thessalonians 5:17, he instructed the Church to "pray without ceasing." Luke 18:1 says, "Men ought always to pray, and not to faint."

It is not enough to know that we should pray. We need to know why. Look at Ephesians 4:14-16:

> That we henceforth be no more children, tossed to and fro, and carried about with every wind of doctrine, by the sleight of men, and cunning craftiness, whereby they lie in wait to deceive; but speaking the truth in love, may grow up into him in all things, which is the head, even Christ: from whom the whole body fitly joined together and compacted by that which every joint supplieth, according to the effectual working in the measure of every part, maketh increase of the body unto the edifying of itself in love.

Compare the Body of Christ to a brick building. The bricks would topple if they were not joined together. Mortar forms those bricks into a solid, impenetrable wall. It is held together, or made useful, by the effectual working of every part. In the same way, the power of love, through prayer and intercession, is the mortar which knits the Body of Christ together. Each member, or "brick," contributes his part by building up the Body and strengthening it through prayer. If one is injured, or weakened in some way, the others are able to stand in prayer and make up for that weakness.

Prayer and Fellowship

It pleases God to answer your prayers. But He can only manifest Himself in the earth through the believer who is operating in faith. Faith makes prayer effective and it pleases God (Hebrews 11:6). However, there will be no strong faith without deep and intimate fellowship with the Father. This is the very heart of a successful prayer life.

Fellowship is the mother of faith because you can only put your faith and confidence in God to the extent you know Him. Just as in any relationship, spending time in fellowship with your heavenly Father is the only way to become personally acquainted with Him.

Your new birth into the family of God has given you the right to expect your prayers to be answered. You have come into a Father-child relationship. Relationship without fellowship, however, is like marriage without love. In a loveless marriage, two people are related but don't really know each other.

If I never spent quality time fellowshiping with my son, anyone could tell him lies about me and he would believe them. The same thing applies to a husband and wife, an employer and employee, business partners, etc. Lack of fellowship causes lack of trust. If this can happen in human relationships, it can happen between you and your heavenly Father.

When I don't know my heavenly Father, Satan can lie to me about Him—trying to convince me He is my problem, or the One making me sick to teach me something. It would be easy to believe him, but my trust (faith) in my Father causes me to refuse Satan's lies (called doubt or unbelief). Isaiah 26:3 says, "Thou wilt keep him in perfect peace, whose mind is stayed on thee: because he trusteth in thee."

The more you fellowship with God, the more you will know He is *not* your problem. He is for you and wants to use His power in your behalf. Galatians 1:3-4 says, "Grace be to you and peace from God the Father, and from our Lord Jesus Christ, who gave himself for our sins, that he might deliver us from this present evil world, *according to the will of God* and our Father."

The No. 1 priority in God's heart is to spend quality time with us daily. We need to be able to hear His voice and follow the promptings of His Holy Spirit. We have the command to resist anything that does not come from Him (James 4:7). He does not want us lacking in any area of our lives.

Let's look at 1 Corinthians 1:4-9:

> I thank my God always on your behalf, for the grace of God which is given you by Jesus Christ; that in every thing ye are enriched by him, in all utterance, and in all knowledge; even as the testimony of Christ was confirmed in you: so that ye come behind in no gift; waiting for the coming of our Lord Jesus Christ: who shall also confirm you unto the end, that ye may be blameless in the day of our Lord Jesus Christ. God is faithful, by whom ye were called unto the fellowship of his Son Jesus Christ our Lord.

When you heed the call to fellowship, you will find out for yourself that God is faithful. Your life will be enhanced by Him. You will not come behind in any area. When you know Him through fellowship you will operate out of your spirit, where the faith and power of God reside. Operating in mere head knowledge of the Word, or "mental assent," will keep you from tapping in to the power of God. Mental assent simply agrees that God's Word is true. But revelation knowledge resulting from consistent and close fellowship with God brings you to a place where you know, that you know, that you know, that His promise is good. Nothing can take revelation knowledge away from you! All fear and doubt is dispelled and you will bear abundant fruit in your life.

Jesus said,

> Abide in me, and I in you. As the branch cannot bear fruit of itself, except it abide in the vine; no more can ye, except ye abide in me. I am the vine, ye are the branches: He that abideth in me, and I in him, the same bringeth forth much fruit: For without me ye can do nothing.... If ye abide in me, and my words abide in you, ye shall ask what ye will, and it shall be done unto you. Herein is my Father glorified, that ye bear much fruit; so shall ye be my disciples (John 15:4-5, 7-8).

Bearing fruit is doing the works of Jesus, consequently pleasing the Father.

Hebrews 13:20-21 says, "Now the God of peace...make you perfect in every good work to do his will, working in you that which is wellpleasing in his sight...." This is a clear example of God's will for every believer.

Notice Colossians 1:9-10: "We...do not cease to pray for you, and to desire that ye might be filled with the knowledge of his will in all wisdom and spiritual understanding; that ye might walk worthy of the Lord unto all pleasing, being fruitful in every good work, and increasing in the knowledge of God." The better you know God, the more fruitful you become through His power working in you.

Fruit bearing comes through prayer. Jesus always separated Himself from people to spend time in prayer. Spending time with the Father in fellowship and prayer kept Him in tune with the Holy Spirit.

Set aside time each day with your heavenly Father. Make the decision you will not allow anything to interfere with your quality time alone with Him.

The more time you spend in God's presence, the more you will act and think like Him. He has already given you His nature. Fellowshiping with Him will cause your desires, attitudes, actions and beliefs to line up with His. Then, when you pray, you will simply be voicing His will. The reality of God will burn into your consciousness. You will not be crying out to a God who is 92 million miles away. He will be right there—closer than a brother. As you draw nigh to God, He will draw nigh to you (James 4:8). No danger, no circumstance, no problem in this world can come near you with God Almighty by your side!

Fellowshiping with God will give birth to a deep, strong faith and trust in His ability. Your prayer life will take on new meaning.

As a born-again believer, you have everything you need to succeed in this life. God is a winner! You are His very own child. You have been born again to win! When you pray in faith and confidence, all of heaven's resources are at your disposal! Determine in your heart you will maintain consistent, intimate fellowship with God so your prayer life will be based on personal knowledge of Him.

Chapter 2
Praying for Results

The major cause of failure in Christian enterprises is a lack of prayer.

Whether your goal is to witness to one man or to preach the gospel to nations, you will succeed or fail based entirely on your prayer life. One percent of your time spent in prayer will produce only 1 percent results. Eighty percent prayer will bring 80 percent results. This formula works every time. The obvious question is, "But how can I expect to receive 100 percent results? I can't spend all my time in prayer." Yes, you can!

Prayer is an attitude. It involves more than just making requests. It is communicating with God. You can live in an attitude of prayer every moment, being in constant communion and fellowship with your heavenly Father.

In order to get results in prayer, you must be convinced that God wants to answer your prayers. In fact, He is as ready and willing to answer you as He was to answer Jesus during His earthly ministry. This may be difficult to believe, but it is true.

I remember how amazed I was to learn about God's willingness to answer my prayers because I had always thought of myself as unworthy. Why would God bother to answer *my* prayers? Ignorance of His Word kept me from receiving His best in my life.

Once I realized the importance of the Word of God, my attitude changed. I realized God does not see His children as unworthy. Notice how Jesus prayed: "...that the world may know that thou hast sent me, *and hast loved them, as thou hast loved me*" (John 17:23). Just think! God loves you and me as much as He loves Jesus! We *are* worthy!

Knowing God is ready to answer your prayers will make you serious about your prayer life. Because you are a child of God, you have an open invitation from Him to come into the throne room at any time.

Never take this prayer privilege lightly. You do not have to enter His presence crawling on your hands and knees. You can boldly stand before God without a sense of guilt, shame or condemnation. Hebrews 4:16 says, "Let us therefore come boldly unto the throne of grace, that we may obtain mercy, and find grace to help in time of need."

What Is Prayer?

Prayer is not an emotional release or an escape valve. It is much more than just asking God for a favor. Most important, prayer is not a religious exercise.

You should be getting results each time you pray. God responds to faith. So just repetition and beautiful words do not get the ear of God. Jesus said in Matthew 6:7, "But when ye pray, use not vain repetitions, as the heathen do: for they think that they shall be heard for their much speaking."

Let me give you an example from my own experience.

Not long after I became a Christian, I asked a minister to pray for me. I was expecting to hear a long, beautiful prayer— one that would cause people to fall on their knees in repentance before God! What I heard was just the opposite. He laid his hand on my chest, bowed his head, and said, "Lord, bless him. Meet his every need." He then turned and walked away. I was left standing there thinking, *How could he do that to me? I have big problems. It should have taken at least 20 minutes of hard praying to cover everything.*

The major difference separating that minister and me was the degree of faith at work in our lives. He was operating in faith, praying exactly what he meant. I was a baby Christian, looking for a physical manifestation of some kind.

The length of time or how hard you pray makes no difference.

When you pray in faith, you have confidence in God's willingness to use His power to answer your prayer.

The man who has confidence in God is very difficult to defeat. He knows, regardless of what comes, he can pray and God will move in his behalf. The key then, to success in prayer, is expecting results. Many Christians think, *I'll pray and maybe something will happen.* They say, "I'm just hoping and praying."

If you are only hoping to get results, you will never receive from God. "Hoping to get" is not the same as "believing you receive." The promises of God bring hope in hopeless situations. However, hope has no substance by itself. "I hope to get healed someday." You hope to receive someday, but someday never comes. Faith brings hope into reality and gives it substance. Hebrews 11:1 says, "Now faith is the substance of things hoped for, the evidence of things not seen." The object of hope becomes a reality through faith. Hope is always in the future. Faith is always now.

Faith causes you to receive from God. The believer who is operating in faith believes God's power went to work the moment he prayed.

God's Word in Prayer

The No. 1 rule in praying for results is to base your prayer on God's Word. It can be relied on just as you would depend on the word of your best friend. If you trust him, you will believe what he says. Faith in God operates the same way. God's Word is the integrity of God Himself (John 17:17).

As an example, let's use the prayer for salvation. The first step is to go to the Word and find out what God says you must do to be saved. Romans 10:9-10 says, "That if thou shalt confess with thy mouth the Lord Jesus, and shalt believe in thine heart that God hath raised him from the dead, thou shalt be saved. For with the heart man believeth unto righteousness; and with the mouth confession is made unto salvation."

Make this scripture the basis of your prayer. Confess with your mouth Jesus as Lord, and believe in your heart that God has raised Him from the dead. God's Word says it, so you can accept it as fact. When you fulfill these two prerequisites, the Word says, "Thou shalt be saved." You must receive it by faith.

When you pray the prayer of salvation, you may not feel different. Realize that your feelings do not have anything to do with it. God's Word is His part of your prayer life. He has already said in His Word, "Thou shalt be saved." You have allowed the Word of God to engineer your prayer. It makes no difference how you feel. Exercise your faith. By the authority of God's Word you are saved! In Mark 11:24 Jesus said, "What things soever ye desire, when ye pray, believe that ye receive them, and ye shall have them."

God's Word is His will. When you pray in line with the Word, you have automatically prayed in line with God's will. First John 5:14-15 says, "And this is the confidence that we have in him, that, if we ask any thing according to his will, he heareth us: And if we know that he hear us, whatsoever we ask, we know that we have the petitions that we desired of him." Your prayer for salvation, based on God's Word, was clearly heard by the Father. After you pray and receive your salvation by faith, you then simply thank God for it.

Second Corinthians 5:17 says, "If any man be in Christ, he is a new creature: old things are passed away; behold, all things are become new." Based on what the Word says, see yourself as a new creation. Visualize that the man you once were died the death of the Cross and was raised to new life by the power of the Holy Spirit (Romans 6:4). This is actually what happened. You prayed according to the Word of God, therefore you are saved.

Praying for healing involves the same faith principles. Search God's Word for your answer. Isaiah 53:5 says, "But he was wounded for our transgressions, he was bruised for our iniquities: the chastisement of our peace was upon him; and with his stripes we are healed." Matthew 8:17 says, "Himself took our infirmities, and bare our sicknesses." Undoubtedly, healing is God's will. According to these scriptures, Jesus paid the full price—not only for sin, but for sickness, disease and the consequences of sin.

More religious traditions have discounted God's will for healing than discredit salvation. To know God's will about healing, look at Jesus. He said, "He that hath seen me hath seen the Father" (John 14:9). During His time on earth, Jesus was the express image of God (Hebrews 1:3). What did He do? He healed the sick. Acts 10:38 says, "God anointed Jesus of Nazareth with the Holy Ghost and with power: who went about doing good, and healing *all* that were oppressed of the devil; for God was with him."

The prayer for healing is a simple one. Say, "Father, in the Name of Jesus, I see in Your Word that healing belongs to me. I believe I receive it. I thank You for it. I act on it now." Once you have prayed...*trust.* Do not let Satan convince you that you are still sick. He will try his best to sell you his lies. Stand your ground! Say, "Satan, it is written...." Then speak what God's Word says about your healing. Just as he fled at the command of Jesus' words, Satan will have to flee when you speak God's Word in faith (Matthew 4:1-11). He has no defense against the Word of God when it is spoken in faith by a believer.

Applying Faith in Prayer

When you begin your prayer based on God's Word, you are starting with the answer. The Word contains the answer to every problem that could confront you.

The next step in praying effectively is found in Mark 11:24. Jesus said, "What things soever ye desire, when ye pray, believe that ye receive them, and ye shall have them." This places a qualification on your prayer. You must believe you receive when you pray. Don't wait until the manifestation comes to believe you receive.

This will seem very difficult at first. But as you get to know God personally, you will become convinced His Word is true. The problem area will diminish. Make a quality decision to believe God's Word. Numbers 23:19 says, "God is not a man, that he should lie; neither the son of man, that he should repent: hath he said, and shall he not do it? or hath he spoken, and shall he not make it good?" You can trust His integrity. When you pray, all you have to do is apply your faith.

Where does faith come from? How do you get it? Romans 10:17 says faith comes by hearing, and hearing by the Word of God. Every believer is dealt the measure of faith (Romans 12:3). He must develop that faith by spending time in the Word of God. The application of your faith, in any given situation, is directly related to your knowledge of God. You could not have faith to be saved before you knew it was God's will to save you. If you feel you need more faith, realize that you already have it. What you need is a more personal knowledge of God, through time in His Word.

Once you have prayed in faith, hold fast to your confession. God is aware of your situation. His power went to work the instant you prayed in faith. You can now rest assured that what you prayed will come to pass. Maintain your faith by keeping your confession—what you say—in line with the Word.

There remaineth therefore a rest to the people of God. For he that is entered into his rest, he also hath ceased from his own works, as God did from his. Let us labour therefore to enter into that rest, lest any man fall after the same example of unbelief. For the word of God is quick, and powerful, and sharper than any twoedged sword, piercing even to the dividing asunder of soul and spirit, and of the joints and marrow, and is a discerner of the thoughts and intents of the heart. Neither is there any creature that is not manifest in his sight: but all things are naked and opened unto the eyes of him with whom we have to do. Seeing then that we have a great high priest, that is passed into the heavens, Jesus the Son of God, let us hold fast our profession (Hebrews 4:9-14).

Speak only words that agree with what you desire. Jesus is seated at the right hand of the Father. As your High Priest, He is seeing to it that the whole system works the way God said it would!

The importance of speaking right words cannot be measured. Faith is released with the mouth. Words are the vehicles. God spoke faith-filled words when He created the universe. Hebrews 11:3 says, "Through faith we understand that the worlds were framed by the word of God...." God spoke and the Spirit of God used the faith in those words to create the worlds.

Jesus released power in His earthly ministry through words. At the tomb of Lazarus, Jesus said, "Lazarus, come forth," and he did. At the city of Nain, Jesus stopped a funeral procession and said, "Young man, I say unto thee, arise." The boy was raised from the dead. Matthew 8:16 says Jesus cast out the devil with His Word. Psalm 107:20 says God sent His Word and it healed the children of Israel.

Words carry power. The very forces of life and death are

powered by the tongue (Proverbs 18:21). Ask the Holy Spirit to reveal to you the importance of speaking right words.

When faith words are spoken, they must be backed by corresponding actions. James 2:17, *The Amplified Bible,* says, "So also faith, if it does not have works (deeds and actions of obedience to back it up), by itself is destitute of power (inoperative, dead)." God's Word instructs us to be doers of what it says and not hearers only. In applying faith, two elements are involved: words and actions. Real Bible faith demands action.

You have to act by faith, not according to your feelings or reasonings. Faith is based on eternal truth and is more dependable than the evidence of your physical senses. According to 2 Corinthians 4:18, we are not to look at things which are seen, but at things which are not seen. The things which are visible are *temporal,* or changeable. The things which are invisible are eternal—they never change. Don't focus your attention on what you perceive through your five physical senses. Keep your heart fixed on the Word of God. Then what you see will come in line with the Word.

To believe God's Word, rather than physical circumstances, is to talk and act the answer instead of the problem. Acting on the Word puts faith in motion. You cannot expect results from your prayer without the operation of faith.

An incident that occurred during the ministry of Jesus is a fine example of faith in action. Jesus was teaching in a private home. The crowd was so large there was no room for anyone else. Some men had brought a sick friend to Jesus to be healed. They could not reach Him because of the crowd, but they refused to be denied. They knocked a hole in the roof and lowered their friend into the room on a stretcher!

The owner of that house thought as much of his roof as you think of yours. How do you suppose he reacted when they tore that hole in his roof? But these men had only one thing in mind—to reach Jesus. They put aside their own dignity and refused to fear the owner of the house or the people around them. When they lowered the sick man into the room, Luke 5:20 says Jesus *saw* their faith. The invisible force of faith became visible through their actions! In response to faith, Jesus forgave the man's sins and healed his body.

What Jesus did 2,000 years ago, He will do today. He is the same yesterday, today and forever (Hebrews 13:8).

Once you have prayed, hold fast to your confession. Refuse to speak contrary to the Word of God. Do not allow circumstances to sway you. Act as though it were already done.

When you apply your faith accurately, according to God's Word, you will get results. You will experience Hebrews 4:16 for yourself. "Let us therefore come boldly unto the throne of grace, that we may obtain mercy, and find grace to help in time of need." It does not say, "Come and hope to get." It says, "Come and obtain!"

A very misunderstood concept, throughout the religious world, is that it is extremely difficult to get God to answer prayer at all—much less answer all prayer. That is a lie of Satan and absolutely contrary to the Word of God. When you believe God's Word in your heart, and pray in line with His Word, you have every right to expect your prayer to bring results. Jesus said, "Verily I say unto you, If ye have faith, and doubt not, ye shall not only do this which is done to the fig tree, but also if ye shall say unto this mountain, Be thou removed, and be thou cast into the sea; it shall be done. And all things, whatsoever ye shall ask in prayer, believing, ye shall receive" (Matthew 21:21-22).

If God will answer the prayer of a sinner to be saved, He will certainly answer the prayers of born-again believers who come to Him in faith concerning their lives.

Refusing Doubt

Satan uses doubt with great skill and cunning to cause you to fail. He knows the importance of getting you to waver. He constantly tries to throw doubt and unbelief into your consciousness. If you begin to wonder whether you have the answer, Satan will purpose to secure a foothold in your mind. By gradually increasing his influence, he knows your faith will become ineffective and cause you to be defeated.

Matthew 14:24-31 is a perfect illustration. Jesus' disciples were traveling to the other side of the sea by ship.

> But the ship was now in the midst of the sea, tossed with waves: for the wind was contrary. And in the fourth watch of the night Jesus went unto them, walking on the sea. And when the disciples saw him walking on the sea, they were troubled, saying, It is a spirit; and they cried out for fear. But straightway Jesus spake unto them, saying, Be of good cheer; it is I; be not afraid. And Peter answered him and said, Lord, if it be thou, bid me come unto thee on the water. And he said, Come. And when Peter was come down out of the ship, he walked on the water, to go to Jesus. But when he saw the wind boisterous, he was afraid; and beginning to sink, he cried, saying, Lord, save me. And immediately Jesus stretched forth his hand, and caught him, and said unto him, O thou of little faith, wherefore didst thou doubt?

When Peter cried out to Jesus, He answered him with one word, *Come*. That command carried the authority necessary to defy all natural power. Faith supported Peter on the water. He stepped out of the boat into a supernatural experience.

When he saw the wind, however, he became afraid and failed. He saw, he feared, and he sank!

Three elements are always involved in defeat:

SEE + FEAR + DOUBT = DEFEATED FAITH

Doubt was the thief that robbed Peter of God's best. Great sermons have been made about how Jesus was there to save him. God's best was not that he be rescued in the nick of time before being overwhelmed by a raging sea! Peter had an opportunity to walk in the supernatural, in spite of what was happening in the natural. Faith or fear—you cannot function in both at the same time. Doubt causes defeat!

In praying effectively, a vital part of your success is knowing how to refuse doubt, fear and unbelief. If you are concentrating on your circumstances instead of the Word, you are building an inner image of the problem and not the solution. What you see on the inside will determine your attitude. If all you envision is your negative circumstances, you will doubt God's Word. Satan will then be able to take advantage of you to thwart your faith process.

Doubt operates in the mental realm. God's Word operates in the spiritual realm. Our responsibility is to use the spiritual weapons at our disposal. Second Corinthians 10:3-5 says, "For though we walk in the flesh, we do not war after the flesh: (For the weapons of our warfare are not carnal, but mighty through God to the pulling down of strong holds;) casting down imaginations, and every high thing that exalteth itself against the knowledge of God, and bringing into captivity every thought to the obedience of Christ." In Matthew 14, Peter's battle was not with natural forces. The combat was spiritual. Natural law was subject to the power inherent in Jesus' word, "Come." By stepping out of the boat, Peter acted on the authority in that word.

We can walk in the supernatural in spite of life's storms raging against us. Our spiritual weapons are mighty!

Do not allow doubt or fear to enter your consciousness. Maintain control of your mind. Be ready to refuse any thought or imagination contrary to your prayer. When doubt comes, refuse to give it any place. Be selective about the thoughts you entertain. Do not build inner images of defeat! You can control your thought life according to Philippians 4:6-9. Learn to think on things that are true, honest, just, pure, lovely and of good report.

Satan uses doubt and fear to bluff you into accepting defeat. But you can overcome him by the power of God and faith in His Word.

Prepare to Succeed

You can avoid failure by preparing to succeed. Once you have prayed in faith, you must stand your ground until the manifestation comes. Fight the good fight of faith. Stand firm on the Word and believe God for results. Give Him the opportunity to do something with your circumstances. God is on your side! Prepare to succeed, not to fail.

When you pray in Jesus' Name, according to the Word in faith, God will quickly respond to you (John 16:23).

Suppose you prayed for healing. Then you think, *What will I do if God doesn't heal me? Maybe I had better make an appointment with the doctor. He's awfully busy this time of year. I might not be able to see him. Then if God doesn't heal me and I don't have an appointment, I'll be in a mess!*

With that attitude, praying is a waste of time. The person who thinks that way will be unable to receive from God. Before he prays, he is already preparing to fail. He is double-minded and, according to James 1:8, unstable in all his ways. He is wavering in his mind and will never receive from God. He is like a wave of the sea, driven with the wind and tossed about in every direction. He has a backup plan "just in case." The moment he feels the least bit sick, he will operate in fear and unbelief. When he feels well, he will act in faith, but he will never achieve any concrete results.

If the thought comes, *What am I going to do if I fail?*, don't give place to it. If you have a setback, just get back on the Word of God. The power of God is the same whether you feel like it or not. Receive the Word into your heart. Renew your mental attitude to the Word. Prepare to succeed, and you'll receive the manifestation in the physical realm.

You may ask, "But how do I prepare to succeed?" Keep your attention on God's Word. Look at Proverbs 4:20-22: "My son, attend to my words; incline thine ear unto my sayings. Let them not depart from thine eyes; keep them in the midst of thine heart. For they are life unto those that find them, and health to all their flesh."

Don't listen to the voice of circumstances around you. Keep the Word of God before you. Do whatever is necessary to keep Satan and circumstances under your control. If that means reading the Word 200 times a day, then do it!

Jesus said in Matthew 6:22, "The light of the body is the eye: if therefore thine eye be single, thy whole body shall be full of light." Your body responds to what it is "fed" through the eyes. If you are believing God for healing, you must "feed" your consciousness with the Word of God, which will bring healing. Waste no time on useless activities. Be diligent to spend your time in God's Word. The Word of God will make you free. Make plans to succeed!

These principles will bring the desired result, which is the manifestation of answered prayer by God's supernatural power. At that moment, you will have a realization of God's ability from personal experience, not just through another's testimony. This is probably the most exciting thing that can happen. You realize God moved because you prayed and used your faith.

The day Gloria and I were married was a beautiful experience in my life. But even greater than that has been the experiences we have had in believing God together, watching Him move when we pray. To know God sees and cares about us, our family and the circumstances around us, has truly enhanced our lives. You haven't lived until you experience the thrill of watching your prayers come to pass!

Chapter 3
The Battlefield of Prayer

Finally, my brethren, be strong in the Lord, and in the power of his might. Put on the whole armour of God, that ye may be able to stand against the wiles of the devil. For we wrestle not against flesh and blood, but against principalities, against powers, against the rulers of the darkness of this world, against spiritual wickedness in high places. Wherefore take unto you the whole armour of God, that ye may be able to withstand in the evil day, and having done all, to stand. Stand therefore, having your loins girt about with truth, and having on the breastplate of righteousness; and your feet shod with the preparation of the gospel of peace; above all, taking the shield of faith, wherewith ye shall be able to quench all the fiery darts of the wicked. And take the helmet of salvation, and the sword of the Spirit, which is the word of God: praying always with all prayer and supplication in the Spirit... (Ephesians 6:10-18).

Every believer is involved in spiritual warfare. The problems we face are brought about by satanic forces—principalities, powers, rulers of the darkness of this world and wicked spirits in heavenly places. Our responsibility is to use the weapons of our warfare to fight the good fight of faith. What are those weapons? The Name of Jesus, the Word of God, the Holy Spirit and the gifts of the Spirit.

Prayer is the battlefield. The time spent in the Word is the base of supply. The armor described in Ephesians 6 is prayer armor and serves one vital purpose: to combat Satan and win!

Your enemy is not other people. Satan is the source of

all your trouble. He is the troublemaker! Not God. Not your neighbor. Not your co-worker. Some people believe God sends tribulation and trials. But He has provided the weapons and armor to get us *out* of trouble!

In combat, a good strategist knows the importance of cutting the enemy's supply and dividing his troops. Defeat is inevitable. Without food, water and ammunition, it will be only a matter of time until the enemy is in his hands. In fact, all he has to do is sit back and wait. In the same way, if we're not keeping supplied by spending time in the Word and prayer, actively combating Satan, then he can easily overtake us.

Much of our failure in the past has been because of Satan's success in dividing the Church. But thank God, the Body of Christ is coming together throughout the earth. People of all denominational backgrounds are uniting in the power of the Holy Spirit. Denominational barriers are crumbling like the walls of Jericho! Believers are daily discovering, more and more, the power of God available to them. They are putting on their prayer armor, preparing to do battle in the realm of the spirit.

Thank God, we have authority over Satan and his cohorts! We are to be strong in the Lord and in the power of His might, mastering our weapons and using them effectively. If we expect to win the war, we must spend time reinforcing our troops through prayer.

The Whole Armor of God

As a believer, you are a soldier in the army of God. Visualize yourself standing ready for battle with the armor of God protecting you—your loins girt with the truth, the breastplate of righteousness in place, your feet shod with the preparation of the gospel of peace. And *above all,* you are holding the shield of faith to quench *all* the fiery darts of the wicked. The helmet of salvation is on your head and the sword of the Spirit—the Word of God—is in your hand.

You are covered from head to foot with the powerful armor of God. It is strong and will withstand any onslaught of the enemy. Let me show you how it works.

When Satan tells you in your mind that you will never see the manifestation of your prayers, it is time to gird yourself with the truth. Ephesians 6:13-14 says, "...And having done all, to stand. Stand therefore, having your loins girt about with truth." In John 17:17 Jesus said, "Thy word is truth." Satan is a liar and the father of lies.

Determine in your heart that having done all to stand, you *will* stand firm on God's Word. You will not be moved by what you see, hear or think. You are only moved by the Word of God.

Psalm 112:6-8 says of the man who delights in God's Word, making it final authority, "Surely he shall not be moved for ever: the righteous shall be in everlasting remembrance. He shall not be afraid of evil tidings: his heart is fixed, trusting in the Lord. His heart is established, he shall not be afraid, until he see his desire upon his enemies."

Fix your attention on God's Word. Trust only in the Lord and not in the evil reports you hear. Establish your heart in the Word of God!

The breastplate of righteousness has a particular meaning to you as a believer. It was no accident that the Spirit of God chose the breastplate to represent righteousness. Without it, vital areas of a soldier's body are exposed to the enemy. Without righteousness, the vital parts of your prayer life are exposed to Satan.

Righteousness may well be the most misunderstood subject in the New Testament. To the religious mind, it is good moral conduct. However, the true meaning is very different. Righteousness is simply right-standing with God. Because of that right-standing, you have rights and privileges in God's kingdom.

You will become more aware of those rights and privileges as you realize what happens when you make Jesus the Lord of your life. There are two spiritual families: the family of God and the family of the devil.

Colossians 1:12-13 says, "Giving thanks unto the Father, which hath made us meet to be partakers of the inheritance of the saints in light: Who hath delivered us from the power of darkness, and hath translated us into the kingdom of his dear Son."

Jesus said to the Pharisees, "Ye are of your father the devil, and the lusts of your father ye will do. He was a murderer from the beginning, and abode not in the truth, because there is no truth in him. When he speaketh a lie, he speaketh of his own: for he is a liar, and the father of it" (John 8:44).

Ephesians 2:2-3 says, "Wherein in time past ye walked according to the course of this world, according to the prince of the power of the air, the spirit that now worketh in the children of disobedience: among whom also we all had our conversation in times past in the lusts of our flesh, fulfilling the desires of the flesh and of the mind; and were by nature the children of wrath, even as others."

Your faith in Jesus gives you power to become a child of God. When you make Jesus the Lord of your life, your spirit is born again. You no longer belong to Satan's kingdom. As Colossians 1:12-13 says, you are translated into the kingdom of God's dear Son. You are now an heir of God and a joint heir with Jesus Christ! What is His is yours. You have His righteousness! This is your breastplate. It makes you worthy in the sight of God.

As long as you see yourself unworthy, you will not experience answered prayer to any great degree. But an understanding of righteousness will put you on the road to success. You have a right to resist Satan and expect him to flee.

Believers all over the world are learning their rights. They are becoming more and more aware of their position as children of God and joint heirs with Jesus (Romans 8:17). They are taking advantage of the breastplate of righteousness!

The next piece of armor is for your feet. They are to be shod with the preparation of the gospel of peace. Jesus said, "Go ye into all the world, and preach the gospel to every creature" (Mark 16:15). The gospel is the good news that we have peace through Jesus Christ. Isaiah 52:7 says, "How beautiful upon the mountains are the feet of him that bringeth good tidings, that publisheth peace...." Sharing the gospel with others is part of your armor.

The Word says, "Above all, taking the shield of faith." Your shield quenches all the fiery darts of the wicked. First John 5:4 says, "...and this is the victory that overcometh the world, even our faith." Your faith makes you an overcomer and more than a conqueror! "The just shall live by faith" (Romans 1:17). This means your whole life is sustained by your faith in God.

Finally, "Take the helmet of salvation." A helmet is protection for the head. Romans 12:2 says, "And be not conformed to this world: but be ye transformed by the renewing of your mind, that ye may prove what is that good, and acceptable, and perfect, will of God." Satan's battleground is your mind. By keeping your mind renewed to the Word of God, you will protect it from Satan's onslaught of doubt and unbelief. This is closely related to having your loins girt with the truth. Freedom is in the truth. Jesus said, "If ye continue in my word, then are ye my disciples indeed; and ye shall know the truth, and the truth shall make you free" (John 8:31-32). The key is continuing. You cannot just try this. You must make a quality decision to do it. You will then experience the freedom from Satan that is rightfully yours as a child of God.

Your armor is the same spiritual armor Jesus wore during His earthly ministry. "And he saw that there was no man, and wondered that there was no intercessor: therefore his arm brought salvation unto him; and his righteousness, it sustained him. For he put on righteousness as a breastplate, and an helmet of salvation upon his head; and he put on the garments of vengeance for clothing, and was clad with zeal as a cloak" (Isaiah 59:16-17). Jesus proved this armor before He gave it to you. It worked proficiently for Him. Why? Because He was here for one purpose—to fulfill God's will in the earth.

Jesus ministered on earth as a prophet under the Abrahamic covenant. Philippians 2:8 says that Jesus humbled Himself to come to earth. In the original Greek it literally says He emptied Himself of His divine privileges. Jesus walked as a man, filled with the Holy Spirit. He said, "I can of mine own self do nothing: as I hear, I judge: and my judgment is just; because I seek not mine own will, but the will of the Father which hath sent me" (John 5:30). He wore the armor, as a man, and then gave it to the Church!

God has set in motion a security system on earth called "prayer." It includes the whole armor of God and the weapons of our warfare. The principles involved are designed to put a padlock on Satan's forces and give the Spirit of God an avenue through which He can carry out God's will in the lives of His people.

The Weapons of Our Warfare

The armor we have talked about has been defensive. Let's look at our offensive weapons. Ephesians 6:17 says the Word of God is the sword of the Spirit. To handle your sword skillfully, you need to know how the Word works. It will bring results. Satan will retreat in terror from its blows!

In Mark 4, Jesus compares the Word of God to seed sown in the ground. When you plant seed, it produces a crop. You do not plant corn expecting to grow apples or bananas. When corn is planted, corn will grow. So it is with the Word of God. When you plant the Word in your heart, it will grow and produce.

Your heart—like soil—will produce what is sown in it. Plant seeds of doubt, fear, unbelief and failure and you can expect to produce a crop of doubt, fear, unbelief and failure in your life. You cannot plant seeds of doubt expecting to produce faith. It simply will not work.

The Word is sharper than a two-edged sword, piercing and dividing asunder the soul and the spirit, the joints and the marrow (Hebrews 4:12). The Word goes beyond your intellect. It enters the spirit realm. Only doubt and unbelief will stop it from operating in your behalf. When you plant the Word concerning healing in your heart, you will produce a harvest of healing—if doubt and fear do not enter and ruin your crop.

Jesus said, "The sower soweth the word....but when they have heard, Satan cometh immediately, and taketh away the word that was sown in their hearts" (Mark 4:14-15). You can see from this scripture that Satan comes immediately to steal the Word. You have to guard against his maneuvers. The best way to combat an enemy is to familiarize yourself with his tactics. Once you know how Satan operates, you will be able to defeat him.

When a man plants seed in the ground, he does not go out a few days later and dig it up to see if it is growing. Seeds never produce that way. He has to have faith in the seed's ability to grow and produce.

Faith in the Word works the same way. When you are believing God for healing and the symptoms linger, do not give up and say, "Well, I guess it didn't work for me." That's what Satan would like you to do. You must continually water the ground and cultivate it with the Word until the seed is able to sprout and grow. Don't dig up your seed!

If a farmer placed his seed on a shelf, it would never produce. He must put the seed in its correct environment for the life in it to come forth. The Word must be treated like that seed. If you need healing, then plant the seed of God's Word concerning healing in the correct environment—your heart. When your Bible is left lying on a bookshelf, it will be of no use to you.

Not spending time in the Word when you are fighting a spiritual battle would be like leaving your sword in its sheath while you are on the battlefield. Take your Bible down from the shelf and feed the Word into your heart. Spend time meditating in the Word until the seed of healing can grow and develop and bring forth the desired fruit in your life.

When a seed is planted in the ground and cultivated, it will take root. The shoot will force its way to the surface. When the plant blooms, it will produce many more just like itself. The Word, like a seed, has the power within itself to grow and bear fruit.

Protect the Word until it has time to take root and grow. Rule over your thought life by casting down imaginations that exalt themselves against the Word. To be carnally minded, or sense ruled, is death (Romans 8:6). It will kill you. To be spiritually minded is life and peace. Keep your thoughts on the Word. It is the answer to your problem. You will experience life and peace by keeping the end result on your mind, thus protecting the seed of God's Word. The Word of God works only when it is put to work. James 4:7 says, "Submit yourselves therefore to God. Resist the devil, and he *will* flee from you."

God has provided a strong arsenal for spiritual warfare. The Word is not your only weapon against Satan. Let's look at another one.

In Chapter 1, we discussed briefly that every believer has the privilege of using the Name of Jesus in prayer. When you pray in Jesus' Name, you immediately get the ear of God. At the same time, you also get Satan's attention.

The Name of Jesus carries ultimate authority in the spirit world. Philippians 2:9-10 says, "God also hath highly exalted him, and given him a name which is above every name: That at the name of Jesus every knee should bow, of things in heaven, and things in earth, and things under the earth." In Jesus' Name, the believer has authority to "tread on serpents and scorpions, and over all the power of the enemy" (Luke 10:19). Satan knows the power invested in that Name and he will retreat when it is spoken in faith (James 4:7). One translation says to stand up to the devil and he will turn and run!

Let's look at Hebrews 1:3-4: "Who being the brightness of his glory, and the express image of his person, and upholding all things by the word of his power, when he had by himself purged our sins, sat down on the right hand of the Majesty on high; being made so much better than the angels, as he hath by inheritance obtained a more excellent name than they." If the Name of Jesus is more excellent than that of the angels in good standing with God, how much more would it be than the name of Satan? He is a fallen angel!

Before He ascended into heaven, Jesus commissioned His disciples to go into all the earth. He said, "All power has been given to me in heaven and in earth. Therefore, *you* go into all the earth. *In My Name* lay hands on the sick and they will recover. *In My Name* cast out devils." (See Matthew 28:18-19; Mark 16:17-18.) Just as a wife has power of attorney to use her husband's name, we have been given Jesus' Name to use in combat against Satan. We have authority to speak His Name in His stead.

When Peter and John ministered to the man at the gate

Beautiful, they spoke in the Name of Jesus. Peter said, "Silver and gold have I none; but such as I have give I thee: In the name of Jesus Christ of Nazareth rise up and walk" (Acts 3:6). Later he explained what had happened. Peter said,

> Ye men of Israel, why marvel ye at this? or why look ye so earnestly on us, as though by our own power or holiness we had made this man to walk? The God of Abraham, and of Isaac, and of Jacob, the God of our fathers, hath glorified his Son Jesus.... And his name through faith in his name hath made this man strong, whom ye see and know: yea, the faith which is by him hath given him this perfect soundness in the presence of you all (Acts 3:12-13, 16).

Peter was simply using the authority Jesus had given him only a few days before. The early apostles did not have special power in themselves to do mighty works. Their holiness didn't make them special. They didn't even have the written New Testament. All they could do was speak the Name of Jesus in faith and the Holy Spirit did the mighty works. The fabulous, earthshaking revival of the early Church was sparked by only one commandment: "Go in the Name of Jesus." The power invested in Jesus' Name has never changed.

Most believers know that it is the Name of Jesus that caused them to be saved. The Bible says, "Whosoever shall call upon the name of the Lord shall be saved." He is rich unto those who call upon His Name (Romans 10:12-13). When you call upon someone's name, you are placing a demand on their ability. For instance, when a policeman says, "Halt in the name of the law!" he is being backed by the power of that particular city. It is as if the entire corporate structure of that city is speaking. He is carrying out the power behind the name of the law.

To know how much confidence you can place in a name, you must be able to measure the power behind it. A man writing a check places a demand on his own name. If he has the proper funds in the bank, then there is enough power to meet the demand.

The power backing the Name of Jesus is the power of Almighty God Himself! First John 3:22-23 says, "And whatsoever we ask, we receive of him, because we keep his commandments, and do those things that are pleasing in his sight. And this is his commandment, That we should believe on the name of his Son Jesus Christ, and love one another, as he gave us commandment." We have a commandment to believe on the Name of the Son of God. To believe in His Name is to put demand on His ability. Jesus said, "Whatsoever ye shall ask the Father in my name, he will give it you" (John 16:23). The mighty, powerful Name of Jesus is available to you. Become aware of your right and privilege to use it. Ask the Holy Spirit to engrave the reality of it in your heart. His ministry is to lead you into all truth (John 16:13).

The Name of Jesus is the key to heaven's storehouse. It can do anything Jesus can do. Speaking His Name is standing in His stead. According to Philippians 2:9-11, the entire spectrum of existence—heaven, earth, under the earth—will bow its knee and confess with its mouth that Jesus is Lord to the glory of God the Father. The Name of Jesus is the Name that is above every name. When He was raised from the dead, Jesus inherited the very Name of God (Hebrews 1:4). To measure the power behind His Name, you would have to measure the power of Almighty God. It can't be done. His power is measureless and He wants to use it in our behalf.

God's love motivates Him to use His power. First John 4:16 says, "And we have known and believed the love that God hath to us...." When you believe the love God has for you, you'll begin to realize you have as much right to use the Name of Jesus as anyone else. Believe the love God has for you.

Once you recognize the reality of God's love in your life, you will realize He has not left you defenseless and powerless against evil. God covered the entire spectrum of Satan's existence with the power invested in the mighty Name of Jesus. Use it freely and confidently in the face of your adversary!

Another essential aspect of our spiritual warfare is the Holy Spirit. Before He went to the cross, Jesus promised to send Him. We have armor and weapons, but it is the Holy Spirit who empowers us to use them.

The Holy Spirit is the power of God. The effectiveness of your prayer life depends on the degree of confidence you place in the Holy Spirit. He is the power behind your prayers that enables you to live and walk as God intends—free from sin, sickness, sorrow and death. He dwells within you. You may not be aware of His presence, but He is there. The Holy Spirit fills a vital role in your prayer life. Pray to the Father in Jesus' Name, not to the Holy Spirit. He is in you—creating, energizing, working—to perform the will of God in your life. By operating on the Word of God, you will see the work of the Holy Spirit. He will do exceeding abundantly beyond what we can even ask or think according to the power that is at work within us (Ephesians 3:20). He is that power.

The Holy Spirit is your helper, sent to bear you up. He has come to your aid to give you might in your inner man. He is in you, instantly ready to do the bidding of God and to uphold the Name of Jesus.

The operation of the Holy Spirit should be a reality to you. When you invite Him into your life, you receive more than just an experience. The Holy Spirit of God comes to abide with you forever. He is residing inside you constantly. He is real and wants to help you in your prayer life.

Pray this prayer out loud:

Father, I ask You now to fill me with Your precious Holy Spirit. As He gives me the utterance, I will speak with new tongues, in my own personal prayer language. I will practice praying in tongues, praying in the spirit, daily. I will do my part to exercise my new language and depend on the Holy Spirit to lead and guide me as I grow in You.

Thank You, Father, for filling me with the Holy Spirit. I'm grateful He is living within me. I'll never be the same because of the Holy Spirit dwelling in me.

In Jesus' Name. Amen.

Man's Authority in Prayer

We have seen that God has given us His armor and His weapons to wage spiritual warfare. Why has He done this? So we can win!

Included in this arsenal is the authority given to the Body of Christ. When you know why you have authority over Satan, you will be confident to use that authority. It covers the whole rank and file of Satan's operation: from the lowest principalities to the highest wicked spirits in heavenly places. Not one area of human existence is left uncovered by the blood of Jesus. Here's why:

God gave the earth to man. He made Adam in His image and gave him dominion (Genesis 1:28). God said, "Be fruitful, and multiply, and replenish the earth, and subdue it: and have dominion...." Adam was God's underruler, with authority over all creation. In reflecting on this awesome reality, the psalmist David wrote:

> What is man, that thou art mindful of him? and the son of man, that thou visitest him? For thou hast made him a little lower than the angels, [The Hebrew word for angels is *elohiym,* meaning "God"—Adam was made in the exact likeness of God] and hast crowned him with glory and honor. Thou madest him to have dominion over the works of thy hands; thou hast put all things under his feet (Psalm 8:4-6).

God gave man His Word and His authority. Adam was a free moral agent who determined his own destiny. He chose to disobey God's Word, committed high treason and turned his authority over to Satan. He willfully bowed his knee to a fallen angel. God was obligated by His own Word to Adam and had to honor Adam's choice. Against God's will, Satan became the god of this world (2 Corinthians 4:4).

The consequences of Adam's choice affected the entire human race. Man lost the life and nature of God and his authority over Satan. The nature of Satan—spiritual death— was lodged in his spirit (Romans 5:12), and has passed on to every member of the human race since then. Man was no longer in the family of God. Satan became the illegitimate stepfather of mankind.

To redeem mankind, God had to destroy the union between man and the devil. In Genesis 3:15, God prophesied the coming of the Messiah who would annihilate the devil. Jesus came to the earth for that very reason: to destroy the works of the devil and recapture man's authority (1 John 3:8).

Before the Redeemer came, God dealt with man through the Abrahamic covenant, a contract that enabled Abraham and his descendants to live in the blessings until Jesus, the Messiah, the spotless Son of God, poured out His blood (Genesis 17; Galatians 3:16-17). (Without the shedding of blood there is no remission of sin, Hebrews 9:22.) Abraham's responsibility was to live perfect and upright before God. He was not able to do so because of spiritual death, so God made provision for his failures with the blood of bulls and goats. But the blood of these old covenant sacrifices only covered sin (read Hebrews 9-10). It could not do away with the sin nature.

Then Jesus was born into the earth of a virgin. The Word that God had spoken (Genesis 3:15) became flesh and dwelt among men (John 1:14). Since God was His Father, Jesus had the nature of God in His spirit. He fulfilled the Abrahamic covenant and walked perfect and upright in the sight of God—as a man. Man had been the key figure in the Fall and therefore had to be the key to redemption. The man, Jesus, passed the test Adam failed!

Second Corinthians 5:21 says, "For he [God] hath made him [Jesus] to be sin for us, who knew no sin; that we might be made the righteousness of God in him." Jesus never *committed* sin. He *became* sin for us.

Since Jesus was made to be our sin, He had to pay its penalty. He died both spiritually and physically. This took Him into the regions of the damned where He went in our place. Isaiah 53:6, 10 says it pleased God to lay upon Him all our punishment—sin, sickness, poverty and the entire curse described in Deuteronomy 28:16-68.

The Cross was a mystery to Satan. The Word tells us had Satan known what was happening, he would not have crucified the Lord of glory (1 Corinthians 2:7-8).

Jesus went into hell to free mankind from the penalty of Adam's high treason. Isaiah 53:9 says, "And he made his grave with the wicked, and with the rich in his death...." The Hebrew word for "death" here is plural. Jesus died two

deaths—physical and spiritual. When He was made to be sin,
He was separated from God, thus crying with a loud voice
while hanging on the Cross, "My God, my God, why hast thou
forsaken me?" (Matthew 27:46).

Jesus fulfilled the Abrahamic covenant. He bore our disobedience and became its final sacrifice. His blood did not
merely cover sin, it did away with the very handwriting of the
ordinances that were against us (Colossians 2:14)! Jesus took our
place, spending three horrible days and nights in the bowels of
this earth, buying back our rights and authority, paying the price
for our sin:

> For as Jonas was three days and three nights in
> the whale's belly; so shall the Son of man be three
> days and three nights in the heart of the earth
> (Matthew 12:40).

> Now that he ascended, what is it but that he also
> descended first into the lower parts of the earth?
> (Ephesians 4:9).

> And having spoiled principalities and powers, he
> made a show of them openly, triumphing over them
> in it (Colossians 2:15).

Jesus defeated Satan and his cohorts in their own domain!
God quickened Him (made Him alive) with eternal life.
Romans 6:4 says, "...Christ was raised up from the dead by
the glory of the Father." The power in that life catapulted Him
through three realms. Philippians 2:9-10 says, "Wherefore God
also hath highly exalted him, and given him a name which is
above every name: that at the name of Jesus every knee should
bow, of things in heaven, and things in earth, and things under
the earth." Nothing could stop the plan of redemption.

In Acts 2, Peter preached how Jesus' soul was not left in hell and that David had seen the plan of redemption beforehand and spoken of His resurrection (verse 31). The pains of death could not hold Jesus! The price for sin had been paid.

Hebrews 1:6, 8 says, "And *again,* when he bringeth in the firstbegotten into the world, he saith, And let all the angels of God worship him.... Thy throne, O God, is for ever and ever: a sceptre of righteousness is the sceptre of thy kingdom." Jesus was the firstborn from the dead (Colossians 1:18). He took on Himself the nature of sin, paid the price and was reborn into sonship!

Jesus identified with the human race and became our total substitute, paying an awesome price for our redemption. When we identify with His death, burial and resurrection, we too become reborn into sonship.

That if thou shalt confess with thy mouth the Lord Jesus, and shalt believe in thine heart that God hath raised him from the dead, thou shalt be saved. For with the heart man believeth unto righteousness; and with the mouth confession is made unto salvation (Romans 10:9-10).

But God, who is rich in mercy, for his great love wherewith he loved us, even when we were dead in sins, hath quickened us together with Christ, (by grace ye are saved;) and hath raised us up together, and made us sit together in heavenly places in Christ Jesus: that in the ages to come he might show the exceeding riches of his grace in his kindness toward us through Christ Jesus (Ephesians 2:4-7).

Jesus is now seated at the right hand of the Father expecting

His enemies to be made His footstool. Jesus is the Head and we are His Body. The feet are in the Body. He is expecting His enemies to be put under our feet.

Authority over the devil has been given into the hands of the Body of Christ. That authority in the world of the spirit is backed by the whole plan of redemption!

Though the things we have studied cannot be seen with the natural eye, nevertheless, they are realities in the spirit and must be accepted by faith in God's Word.

Put yourself in Satan's position and see these things from his viewpoint. If you were Satan, what would you think? Standing before you is a soldier, clad in a complete set of God's armor— the breastplate of righteousness, the helmet of salvation, the girdle of truth, the shoes of the gospel of peace, the shield of faith and the sword of the Spirit. This soldier is speaking God's Word with authority. With the face mask pulled down, you could not tell the difference between him and Jesus. If you were Satan, wouldn't you give careful consideration before you jumped into combat with him? This same image already eternally wounded him in defeat. Satan says, "Once is enough. I'll flee!"

The only way a believer reveals himself to Satan is by lifting his faceplate through unbelief. As long as he acts and lives by faith, Satan will be unable to defeat him. In *Wuest's Expanded Translation of the New Testament* James 4:7-8 says, "Be subject with implicit obedience to God at once and once for all. Stand immovable against the onset of the devil and he will flee from you. Draw near to God and He will draw near to you."

You have been given the whole armor of God. Your responsibility is to pick it up, put it on, and wear it in faith. You have the Holy Spirit, the Word of God and the authority in the realm of the spirit. You have been fully equipped with weapons that guarantee results in prayer. Expect those results every time you pray!

Chapter 4
Prayer That Changes Things

Following are types of prayer by which you can change things: (1) the prayer of agreement, (2) binding, (3) loosing, (4) petition and supplication, (5) intercession and (6) united prayer.

Always remember that prayer changes *things*. It doesn't change God. One of the mighty attributes of God is that He is the same yesterday, today and forever (Hebrews 13:8). Use your faith and the Word of God to change the circumstances in your life to line up with His will. His plans and desires are always for your success and well-being.

Some people think if they pray long and hard enough they will get God to do something for them. The Word says God's eyes are over the righteous and His ears are open to their prayers (Psalm 34:15). If you have made Jesus the Lord of your life, you are the righteousness of God in Christ Jesus. He is already open to your prayers. Through prayer, you tap in to His strength and change the things that are out of line with His will.

The Prayer of Agreement

The prayer of agreement when prayed according to Matthew 18:18-20 will cover every circumstance in life:

> Verily I say unto you, Whatsoever ye shall bind on earth shall be bound in heaven: and whatsoever ye shall loose on earth shall be loosed in heaven. Again I say unto you, That if two of you shall agree on earth as touching any thing that they shall ask, it shall be done for them of my Father which is in heaven. For where two or three are gathered together in my name, there am I in the midst of them.

Let me use finances to illustrate. The first thing to do is agree with the Word. Read the scriptures and pray. Gloria and I sometimes write down our agreements like this:

> We hereby agree, according to Philippians 4:19 and Matthew 18:19 as follows: Father, we see in Your Word that You will supply all our needs according to Your riches in glory. We are setting ourselves in agreement that our financial need is met according to Your Word. We believe we receive (be specific) _____. We establish this agreement, in Jesus' Name. Amen.

Amen means "So be it." As far as we are concerned, the matter is closed. We just thank God from that point forward. We know if we want results *we must not waver.* To waver is to doubt.

If Satan brings doubt, we simply speak to him in the authority of Jesus' Name and say, "Don't bring us your lies. Not only is it written in God's Word, but we have agreed. We have written it down." As far as we are concerned, the need is met. There is no doubt about it because we have agreed according to the Word of God. Consequently, our confession and actions will be in line with what we have established as truth.

There have been times when we have wavered, so we take it to God and receive forgiveness for unbelief, reinforce our original decree and go at it again. We all make mistakes in the walk of faith. The important thing is to keep walking. If you miss it, go at it again. The biggest mistake of all is to become discouraged and quit before you receive your answer.

I challenge you to write down your agreements. Seeing it in black and white on paper will make a difference! You will be more likely to line up your confession and your actions with your agreement.

Jesus said that if any two on earth agree, He would be in the midst of that agreement to see that it comes to pass. You are on earth so you qualify. If you agree with another believer as touching anything that lines up with the Word of God, He is there in your midst to carry it out.

Jesus wants you to agree and will see to it that it comes to pass. The word *agree* is translated in *The Amplified Bible* as "agree and harmonize together or make a symphony together." The word *symphony* caught my attention one time, so I looked it up and found that it means "all available instruments in harmony." You must have your spirit, mind and actions in agreement with the Word.

Agreeing spiritually is to agree with the Word of God. Make up your mind God's Word is true and that it will come to pass.

Secondly, be strong in your mind. That is Satan's battleground. You must control your thoughts. Writing down your agreement will be beneficial for this reason. It will keep it before your eyes so when your mind tries to change directions, control it with your agreement on God's Word. Do not tie God's hands. Allow Him to work.

You have agreed, spirit and soul (mind). Then your actions must come in line. If finances are what you agreed on, expect the money to come in. This is part of being in agreement. You cannot agree in prayer about something, then act the opposite and expect it to come to pass. If you do, your actions will eventually take over your thinking.

Agreement with the Word and another believer are not the only things involved in this kind of prayer. Agreement is also harmony.

Harmony is extremely important. When speaking of prayer in Mark 11:25-26, Jesus said, "And when ye stand praying, forgive, if ye have aught against any: that your Father also which is in heaven may forgive you your trespasses. But if ye do not forgive, neither will your Father which is in heaven forgive your trespasses." This is vital in your prayer life. You must forgive everyone who has offended you. Jesus did not say, "Think about it for six weeks and then forgive if or when you feel better." He said, *forgive when you pray*.

Jesus prayed, "Our Father which art in heaven, Hallowed be thy name. Thy kingdom come, Thy will be done in earth, as it is in heaven. Give us this day our daily bread. And forgive us our debts, as we forgive our debtors" (Matthew 6:9-12). He put a condition on forgiveness. The condition is "I don't expect to be forgiven until I forgive." He displayed the kind of discipline the believer should exercise when he is praying.

How important is this? In Galatians 5:6, the Bible says faith works by love. If you are operating with an unforgiving heart, your prayer life will be paralyzed.

The Word says we know we have the petitions we have desired of Him, if we do the things that are pleasing in His sight (1 John 3:22). Put these scriptures together and you quickly see unforgiveness would actually ruin the whole prayer system.

Agreement makes prayer work. You can experience a place of agreement with God's Word, and harmony that will produce power, as you forgive and agree with another believer. You can affect governments, families and the lives of others. You can change your financial situation, affect your church and your pastor with the power of prayer. Find someone who can agree with you according to the Word of God.

The same principle works the other way. If you are in *dis*-agreement, the door is open for Satan to come in. "For where envying and strife is, there is confusion and every evil work" (James 3:16).

In Matthew 18:21-22, Peter asked Jesus, "Lord, how oft shall my brother sin against me, and I forgive him?" till seven times? Jesus replied, "I say not unto thee, Until seven times:

but, Until seventy times seven." *Forgive because God said to, and not because you feel like it.*

Build your home, your church and every other area of your life on the unselfish love of God. Selfishness has never built anything it did not destroy. But love never fails. The love of God is the very center of the family of God because God is love. You are His very own child, born again with His love nature inside you.

Don't let that love lie dormant. Cast down selfishness and let loose the love of God in you. You cannot fail when love is in dominion.

When you forgive and reach for harmony, you come to a place where you have the spiritual awareness to perceive the closeness of God. Jesus said if you get into harmony and agree together, He would be in the midst of you. God wants to be involved with you.

When you are in harmony and agreement with those around you, you will step into a deeper, more personal fellowship with God. He becomes real and vital to you. Fellowship with your heavenly Father is one of the greatest things you will ever have in your Christian walk! It causes a confidence and an assurance deep down in your heart. You know your prayers are answered because you have conformed yourself to His will. As you forgive, the joy that comes through answered prayer will become your own personal experience. Jesus said, "Ask, and ye shall receive, that your joy may be full" (John 16:24).

The Prayer of Binding and Loosing

God intends for the Body of Christ to police the evil forces of this world. We are to change circumstances to line up with God's will and put Satan under our feet through the power of God. We are to spoil his plans, plots and maneuvers against God's people!

The prayer of binding and loosing halts Satan's activities. Matthew 12:29 says, "Or else how can one enter into a strong man's house, and spoil his goods, except he first bind the strong man? and then he will spoil his house." You have authority over Satan (Luke 10:19). You exercise it with the prayer of binding and loosing. "Verily I say unto you, Whatsoever ye shall bind on earth shall be bound in heaven: and whatsoever ye shall loose on earth shall be loosed in heaven" (Matthew 18:18).

As you enforce the authority vested in the Church, speak directly to Satan. Exercise your faith in Jesus' work at Calvary.

When Jesus was raised from the dead, He stripped Satan of his authority over mankind. That authority has been delegated to the Body of Christ in the earth. Bind Satan in the Name of Jesus.

Many times Gloria and I add a paragraph to our agreement prayer: "Satan, we bind you and render you helpless in this situation. As a matter of record, you are hereby bound in the Name of Jesus." From then on, we thank God that Satan is bound and unable to work in the situation. We refuse to give him any place.

The ultimate choice is yours whether or not to receive from God. Jesus asked the man at the pool of Bethesda, "Wilt thou be made whole?" (John 5:6). His attitude is still the same: "Do you want to stay the way you are, or do you want to be made whole?" The choice is yours. God has already provided the way out for you.

Do not give Satan any place by talking about the problem after you have agreed and bound him. Instead of talking the problem, talk the answer—God's Word.

Then loose the angelic forces of God to see that it comes to pass. Hebrews 1:13-14 describes the angels as ministering spirits, sent to minister for them who shall be heirs of salvation. They are messengers sent to work in our behalf. Say: "Ministering spirits, I loose you in the Name of Jesus to minister in my behalf according to the will of God."

The Prayer of Petition and Supplication

The words *petition* and *supplication* are defined as "a formal request addressed to a higher power." This prayer changes things. It is based on Philippians 4:6: "Be careful for nothing; but in every thing by prayer and supplication with thanksgiving let your requests be made known unto God."

To illustrate, suppose you obtained an audience with the governor of your state. After you went through the proper channels, would you then enter his office without being prepared? Of course not! You would have your ideas formulated and the arguments settled in your mind long before you obtained an audience with him. Shouldn't you handle yourself in the same way when approaching God? Hebrews 4:16 says, "Let us therefore come boldly unto the throne of grace...."

Do not go into the prayer of petition and supplication without knowing what you want to say and how you want to say it. Enter the throne room with your petition drawn up according to God's Word. Ask yourself these questions: What happened at Calvary? How did the substitutionary sacrifice of Jesus affect this trial I am facing? Then, find out what God has already done regarding your situation. If you need healing, look up those scriptures pertaining to healing. Present your petition. No matter what your situation may be, God has provided an answer for it in His Word. The Cross paid the price for your deliverance.

United Prayer

So when they had further threatened them, they let them go, finding nothing how they might punish them, because of the people: for all men glorified God for that which was done. For the man was above forty years old, on whom this miracle of healing was shown. And being let go, they went to their own company, and reported all that the chief priests and elders had said unto them. And when they heard that, they lifted up their voice to God with one accord, and said, Lord, thou art God, which hast made heaven, and earth, and the sea, and all that in them is: who by the mouth of thy servant David hast said, Why did the heathen rage, and the people imagine vain things? The kings of the earth stood up, and the rulers were gathered together against the Lord, and against his Christ. For of a truth against thy holy child Jesus, whom thou hast anointed, both Herod, and Pontius Pilate, with the Gentiles, and the people of Israel, were gathered together, for to do whatsoever thy hand and thy counsel determined before to be done. And now, Lord, behold their threatenings: and grant unto thy servants, that with all boldness they may speak thy word, by stretching forth thine hand to heal; and that signs and wonders may be done by the name of thy holy child Jesus. And when they had prayed, the place was shaken where they were assembled together; and they were all filled with the Holy Ghost, and they spake the word of God with boldness (Acts 4:21-31).

In this day and time, united prayer is seldom discussed. But in most instances in the Bible involving a body of believers, we find them praying in a united manner. In many of our churches today, however, someone usually leads in prayer. Very little is taught from the Word about praying together out loud.

The previous scripture is the basis for united prayer. Peter and John had been arrested and appeared before the religious council. Their lives were threatened if they continued to preach in the Name of Jesus. They went back to their own company and told everyone what had happened. When they heard, they all prayed. A tremendous amount of power is involved in united prayer.

What were the results of this prayer? Acts 5:12 says, "And by the hands of the apostles were many signs and wonders wrought among the people...." Their one request was answered exactly the way they prayed. The political system of the day tried, but could not stop the power of God in operation. This united prayer was offered accurately according to the Word of God.

As the Body of Christ, we need to get in one accord on the Word of God and expect results. It will cause things to change!

Chapter 5
Intercessory Prayer

The prayer of intercession is prayed in behalf of others. Through His Word, God has called the Body of Christ to the ministry of intercession.

"I exhort therefore, that, first of all, supplications, prayers, intercessions, and giving of thanks, be made for all men; for kings, and for all that are in authority; that we may lead a quiet and peaceable life in all godliness and honesty. For this is good and acceptable in the sight of God our Saviour; who will have all men to be saved, and to come unto the knowledge of the truth" (1 Timothy 2:1-4).

During a time of fasting, God revealed to me that He is calling the Church to rally around the prayer of intercession. We are to call on Him to pour out of His Spirit in these last days in great, unusual manifestations of His power. God is about to bring forth the grand finale. It will be the greatest production by the Spirit of God in the history of the human race.

We are the most privileged generation to have ever lived on this earth. We are blessed not only to witness these manifestations, but also to be the vessels through which His mighty power will flow.

The miraculous things that occurred in the early Church, as recorded in the book of Acts, will be common among us in these last days. Intercessory prayer is the tool that the Spirit of God will use to bring them into manifestation.

We are entering into the most exciting move of the Holy Spirit the Church has ever experienced. I believe this is the last big thrust to harvest the souls of this world into the kingdom of God.

Why are we called to intercession? Because God does not do anything in the earth without the cooperation of a man.

He intends that we work together with Him to accomplish His will. Man is still in authority in the earth. God put him in that position.

I believe we are the generation that will usher in the coming of the Lord Jesus Christ for His Church. Before He comes, the Spirit of God will be poured out upon all flesh. James 5:7 says, "Behold, the husbandman waiteth for the precious fruit of the earth, and hath long patience for it, until he receive the early and latter rain." John 15:1 tells us the husbandman is the heavenly Father. The fruit of the earth is the harvest of souls (Matthew 9:37-38). The rain is the outpouring of the Holy Spirit (Hosea 6:3).

Intercessory prayer causes the rain of God's Spirit to bring the harvest of the human race into the family of God. Right now, all over the world, God is bringing the Body of Christ into unity. As rivers of living water, believers joined together will cause a flood of God's power in the earth.

Because of the crucial time we are living in, this move of the Holy Spirit is causing believers everywhere to respond to the call to intercession. This world will not take much more sin! Romans 8:22 says all of creation groans for the manifestation of the sons of God. Heaven is reverberating 24 hours a day with the intercession of God's people.

We are at the end of what began on the Day of Pentecost. The Apostle Peter said:

> But this is that which was spoken by the prophet Joel; And it shall come to pass in the last days, saith God, I will pour out of my Spirit upon all flesh: and your sons and your daughters shall prophesy, and your young men shall see visions, and your old men shall dream dreams: And on my servants and on my handmaidens I will pour out in those days of

my Spirit; and they shall prophesy: And I will show wonders in heaven above, and signs in the earth beneath... (Acts 2:16-19).

The result of this outpouring of the Holy Spirit is: "And it shall come to pass, that whosoever shall call on the name of the Lord shall be saved" (verse 21).

In order to be saved, one must be born into the family of God. Jesus said, "Except a man be born again, he cannot see the kingdom of God" (John 3:3). He was speaking of the spiritual new birth. "That which is born of the flesh is flesh; and that which is born of the Spirit is spirit" (verse 6). Intercession is giving birth in the realm of the spirit.

Did you notice the words servants and handmaidens in Acts 2:18? When you are born again, you do not become a servant of God. You become a child of God. In order to become a servant or handmaiden, you must make a choice. *Vine's Expository Dictionary of Biblical Words* says these words mean "one who gives himself up to the will of another." Because of your love for God, you choose to serve Him. You yield your will to His will and become a co-laborer with Him. Those who totally give themselves to His service will be God's mouthpiece in the earth. They will be the vehicles of His Spirit.

The Apostle Paul called himself a servant of Jesus Christ. *Vine's* defines *servant* as being in "subjection without the idea of bondage, the perfect example being Christ Himself." Paul had the right to go free, but didn't. He served his Master out of love and dedication. God is calling us to be His servants. Jesus said that many are called but few are chosen (Matthew 20:16). In other words, few dedicate themselves to servanthood. Upon those and out of those who are dedicated to Him, God will pour out of His Spirit upon all flesh.

Jesus said, "Whosoever drinketh of the water that I shall

give him shall never thirst; but the water that I shall give him shall be in him a well of water springing up into everlasting life" (John 4:14). The Spirit of God is a well of living water inside you, springing up. A well is for personal use. God's ultimate purpose is that other thirsty souls can partake of that water. He desires to pour out of His Spirit from the inside of you through intercession.

"He that believeth on me, as the scripture hath said, out of his belly shall flow rivers of living water" (John 7:38). A river is for everyone's use. The outpouring of the Spirit is a flow of the Holy Spirit coming from inside the believer. That flow is the source of all the signs and wonders and miracles! Everyone—the Scripture says, all flesh—will benefit. Intercessory prayer is going to play the major role in this outpouring. It is what causes God's power to flow in the earth, unhindered.

Prayer is the doorway into the mightiest release of power known to man. It brings the very presence of God to and upon man, in any part of the world. That power operates as believers allow those rivers of living water to gush toward the dry and thirsty. The torrential outpouring of the Spirit will cause life to spring forth in those who receive the seed of God's Word. The result is the harvest of new creatures in Christ Jesus (1 Peter 1:23).

Let's study the art of intercession. Isaiah 59:16-17 says, "And he saw that there was no man, and wondered that there was no intercessor: therefore his arm brought salvation unto him; and his righteousness, it sustained him. For he put on righteousness as a breastplate, and an helmet of salvation upon his head; and he put on the garments of vengeance for clothing, and was clad with zeal as a cloak." What is His arm? Jesus. The sole purpose of Jesus' coming to the earth was to be that intercessor. He wore the helmet of salvation and the breastplate of righteousness. That is the same armor in Ephesians 6 for the Body of Christ. Jesus came as an intercessor. We are to put on that same armor and enter into the same field of prayer. His arm is bringing salvation again. As intercessors, we are His arm in the earth causing reconciliation between men and God. Jesus said, "As my Father hath sent me, even so send I you" (John 20:21). The armor is the same and the calling is the same.

You may say, "Do you mean to tell me that I have the same calling on my life Jesus had?" Absolutely! Second Corinthians 5:18 says we have been given the ministry of reconciliation. Jesus said, "[You] go...into all the world, and [you] preach the gospel to every creature" (Mark 16:15). He also said, "The works that I do shall [you] do also; and greater works than these shall [you] do; because I go unto my Father" (John 14:12). He went, didn't He? Then you and I are responsible for the works. He provided us with the new birth. God said in Ezekiel 36:26 that He would put a new spirit within us. Jesus said in John 14:17 that His Spirit would be in us. That gives us the right and the miraculous power to enter into the intercessory prayer ministry.

Intercession is the highest expression of love. It is loving in the spirit, applying spiritual power for another person. It will overpower the evil influences that have bound that person. Your prayer may be for salvation, healing, or any other area of deliverance from Satan.

Second Corinthians 4:3-4 says, "But if our gospel be hid, it is hid to them that are lost: in whom the god of this world hath blinded the minds of them which believe not, lest the light of the glorious gospel of Christ, who is the image of God, should shine unto them."

Satan has blinded the minds of those who have not received the gospel. Your intercessory prayer wrestles against

evil spirits that have deceived them. It is literally giving yourself, your time, your life for others. Jesus said, "Greater love
hath no man than this, that a man lay down his life for his
friends" (John 15:13). This is the God kind of love. It is unselfish. The world did not know this kind of love until Jesus came
to the earth. He laid down His life to come to earth and live as
a man. He emptied Himself of His divine privileges and fulfilled His earthly ministry as a man, filled with the Holy Spirit.
Philippians 2:7-8 says Jesus "made himself of no reputation,
and took upon him the form of a servant, and was made in
the likeness of men: And being found in fashion as a man,
he humbled himself, and became obedient unto death, even
the death of the cross." Love motivated God to send Him.
"For God so loved the world, that he gave his only begotten
Son, that whosoever believeth in him should not perish, but
have everlasting life" (John 3:16). Jesus' love for the Father
impelled Him to obey. He said, "My meat is to do the will of
him that sent me, and to finish his work" (John 4:34).

Jesus has provided reconciliation between God and man
through His substitutionary sacrifice at Calvary. We are
co-laborers with Him. Redemption was bought with a high
price. Jesus didn't take it lightly and neither should we. God's
heart was hungry for a family. Jesus freely gave Himself for
this desire. What an act of love!

God's heart is still hungry. He yearns for every sinner to be
restored to Himself through the new birth, and every believer
to be in close fellowship with Him.

To give your life means to give everything. Jesus came as an
intercessor and He is still giving Himself in intercession today.
Hebrews 7:25 says, "...he ever liveth to make intercession." We
have said, "Jesus *gave* His life for us." But, He is still giving His
life for us, still interceding. His Body in the earth is wearing the
same prayer armor He wore. We have inherited His armor to

do His work and enter into His ministry of intercession.

We have been given that same love that motivated Jesus to come as the intercessor! Romans 5:5 says the love of God has been shed abroad in our hearts by the Holy Ghost. The love that desires to lay down its own desires, and to intercede for someone else, is abiding on the inside of us! The love that impelled Jesus to go to the cross compels us to intercede. We pray for others so they can come into the knowledge of the truth.

Through the knowledge of God's Word, we realize His love is in us. That love urges us to reach out to others. It urges us to be soul winners. A soul winner is an intercessor in action. Jesus paid the price to win souls. Intercessory prayer softens people's hearts to receive the message of the gospel.

When you are filled with the Holy Spirit, you receive the ability to speak in another language. "And they were all filled with the Holy Ghost, and began to speak with other tongues, as the Spirit gave them utterance" (Acts 2:4). The Holy Spirit gives the utterance and you do the speaking.

Just as your own language is the voice of your mind, praying in tongues is the voice of your spirit. It is your spirit speaking mysteries to God (1 Corinthians 14:2). The Apostle Paul said, "If I pray in an unknown tongue, my spirit prayeth, but my understanding is unfruitful" (1 Corinthians 14:14).

Praying in other tongues is the most valuable tool you have in intercessory prayer. When you pray in other tongues, you operate in the realm of the spirit. The Holy Spirit knows what is needed in the lives of others when you do not know (Romans 8:26). The weapons of your warfare are mighty through *God* to the pulling down of strongholds.

When you move in this area of intercession, your physical man will be your spirit man's assistant. You begin to speak in a language that comes out of the inner man. The Spirit of the living God can speak to your own human spirit and out of it will come rivers of living water. You are not just praying mentally limited prayers. When you pray in tongues, you pray beyond your own limited knowledge. You have moved beyond the natural into the spirit. You must yield to it as an act of your will.

If you are not filled with the Spirit, ask God to fill you right now. Put down this book, ask the Lord to fill you with His Spirit, and then open your mouth and allow your new prayer language to flow.

Your first prayer assignment is not for yourself. It is to pray for all men, for kings and men in high authority (1 Timothy 2:1-4). When you respond to the call of intercession, the Holy Spirit prays the perfect will of God through you.

Separate yourself from the things of this world. Get in your prayer closet alone with God and commit to intercession. Begin praying for a specific body of people: a family, a village, a country, a state or a nation. You do not need to wait for a burden for this. The Word says Jesus was moved with compassion (Matthew 9:36). Compassion is not a feeling, it is a Person. Yield to His love inside you. All the motivation you need will come that way. The One who ever liveth to make intercession is living in you! He's already motivated! Yield to Him.

Isaiah 64:7 says, "And there is none that calleth upon thy name, that stirreth up himself to take hold of thee...." The Spirit of God will not be able to help you intercede unless you are willing to stir yourself and take that position of intercession. Paul told Timothy to stir up the gift that was in him (2 Timothy 1:6). You stir it up!

Begin to pray by making yourself available to the Holy Spirit. Again, yield to Him. Allow Him to use you to pray for the man who does not have anyone to pray for him. Stand in the gap for him. Start where you are and allow it to spread to the world. You are literally fighting spiritual warfare in their behalf. The Apostle Paul said, "For I would that ye knew what great conflict I have for you, and for them at Laodicea, and for as many as have not seen my face in the flesh" (Colossians 2:1). This was the same conflict Paul talked about in Ephesians 6 when he said we wrestle against principalities, powers, rulers of the darkness of this world, and spiritual wickedness in high places (Ephesians 6:12). The family of God is not based on selfishness. It is based on love. Intercession is the highest expression of love.

When you commit yourself to pray for those who need Jesus, remember the Bible says you are going to have to bind Satan in order to spoil his house (Matthew 12:29). You are confronting all the forces of evil that have them bound. Do not stop just because it looks like they will never receive. Your intercession is placing pressure on Satan and his forces. Do not relent, but persevere in prayer. It is up to them to make their own choice. But through your intercession, they will be able to make that choice. They will no longer be blinded by Satan.

Take these scriptures before the Holy Spirit and give Him the opportunity to reveal them to you personally. He is the Teacher. He can show you how they work. You can stir up the gift within you simply by desiring to know how intercession works.

Before spiritual births take place, travail goes forth. In the natural realm, a woman does not give birth without labor. In the spirit, travail is the labor that brings forth the new birth. Intercession is God's heartbeat because it is the labor that births the souls of this world into His family.

We noticed Isaiah 64:7 spoke of stirring oneself up. Isaiah 66:8 says, "Who hath heard such a thing? who hath seen such things? Shall the earth be made to bring forth in one day? or shall a nation be born at once? for as soon as Zion travailed, she brought forth her children." Let's find out who Zion is and what she does to travail, and how the children are brought in.

Hebrews 12:22-23 says, "But ye are come unto mount Zion, and unto the city of the living God, the heavenly Jerusalem, and to an innumerable company of angels, to the general assembly and church of the firstborn, which are written in heaven, and to God the Judge of all, and to the spirits of just men made perfect." Zion is the Church of the firstborn. Jesus is the firstborn of many brethren (Romans 8:29). Zion is the Church of Jesus Christ. If you are a member of the Body of Christ, you are Zion.

In Galatians 4:19 Paul said, "My little children, of whom I travail in birth again...." If he is travailing in birth again, he must have travailed before to bring the children to birth.

Travail causes others to be born again. Why would the Scriptures compare intercession to birth? Jesus said out of the belly, the deepest interior of a man, would flow these rivers of living water (John 7:38). So stir yourself up and start praying in other tongues! Your spirit is praying. Keep at it. Soon you will notice the Holy Spirit will take hold together with you. You will begin to travail as if in labor.

You may groan out loud. You are releasing spiritual power. The Word says, "The effectual fervent prayer of a righteous man availeth much" (James 5:16). *The Amplified Bible* translation says, "The earnest (heartfelt, continued) prayer of a righteous man makes tremendous power available [dynamic in its working]." This is the art of intercession. It is stirring yourself up to take hold with the Holy Spirit to cause eternal changes in the lives of others.

Romans 8:26 says, "Likewise the Spirit also helpeth our infirmities...." The word *helpeth* is translated from three Greek words which together mean "takes hold together with us against." That verse literally reads: "Likewise the Spirit also [takes hold together with us against] our infirmities: for we know not what we should pray for as we ought: but the Spirit itself [or Himself] maketh intercession for us with groanings which cannot be uttered. And he that searcheth the hearts knoweth what is the mind of the Spirit, because he maketh intercession for the saints according to the will of God" (verses 26-27). He is telling the Body of Christ about the forces available through intercession. The Holy Spirit sees to it that God's will is carried out even in areas where we do not know how to pray. He searches the heart and knows the mind of the spirit of a man. In other words, you can go beyond your own mental ability and knowledge.

God's purpose is for us to begin to pray for one another. Intercession gives the Holy Spirit the opportunity to bring the fullness of God's will to pass in the earth.

Chapter 6
Kinds of Prayer

"Stand therefore....praying always with all prayer and supplication in the Spirit..." (Ephesians 6:14, 18).

God's Word instructs us to "pray always with all prayer." Other translations say, "all kinds of prayer" or "different kinds of prayer." *The Amplified Bible* says, "with all [manner of prayer]." There is more than just one kind of prayer, depending on what you desire from the Lord. Let's discuss each one in the light of God's Word.

Prayer of Dedication and Worship

Then cometh Jesus with them unto a place called Gethsemane, and saith unto the disciples, Sit ye here, while I go and pray yonder. And he took with him Peter and the two sons of Zebedee, and began to be sorrowful and very heavy. Then saith he unto them, My soul is exceeding sorrowful, even unto death: tarry ye here, and watch with me. And he went a little farther, and fell on his face, and prayed, saying, O my Father, if it be possible, let this cup pass from me: nevertheless not as I will, but as thou wilt (Matthew 26:36-39).

The prayer of dedication and worship holds a tremendous amount of power. We need to know how it works and when it is to be used. In the past, it has been misunderstood. When the leper came to Jesus and said, "I know You can make me well...if You will," Jesus said, "I will." He already knew the Father's will was healing. He did not have to pray, "If it be Thy will." God's will is to be done on earth as it is in heaven

(Matthew 6:9-10). Heaven has no sickness.

The only time the word "if" would *not* be an expression of unbelief is in the prayer of dedication and worship. All other times, using the word "if" in prayer can create unbelief. Praying for healing then, whether it be yours or someone else's, is a prayer that changes things so do not use "If it be Thy will."

Unbelief hinders prayer. Most people pray, "If it be Thy will," thinking they are being humble. Actually, they are praying in ignorance of the Word of God.

The prayer of dedication is getting your will in line with God's will to bring success into a situation. It joins you and God, and aims you toward the same goal. So many times people are running in the opposite direction, hoping God is going to support their endeavors. You should get God involved with those endeavors before you ever move! Never be afraid to yield your will to God. He wants you to succeed! His will is always to your advantage. Proverbs 16:3 in *The Amplified Bible* says, "Roll your works upon the Lord [commit and trust them wholly to Him; He will cause your thoughts to become agreeable to His will, and] so shall your plans be established and succeed."

When you pray the prayer of dedication and live by it, you will experience the peace of God because you are truly trusting Him. Isaiah 26:3 says, "Thou wilt keep him in perfect peace, whose mind is stayed on thee: because he trusteth in thee."

Thanksgiving and Praise

The Bible says if you pray according to God's will, you know He hears you and you have the petitions you desired of Him (1 John 5:14-15). God's Word is His will.

God is faithful. His Word can be relied on. Don't wait until you can see the manifestation before you believe you have it. That will put you over into an area of waiting and hoping. If you believe you receive when you pray, begin to praise God for the answer.

Faith involves thanksgiving and praise. Philippians 4:6 says, "Be careful for nothing; but in every thing by prayer and supplication with thanksgiving let your requests be made known unto God." Thanksgiving and praise are integral parts of prayer.

You and God are working together. It is your prayer and His power.

Praise is more than just words. There is power in it. God did not ordain praise just so we could brag on Him. Psalm 8:1-2 says, "O Lord our Lord, how excellent is thy name in all the earth! who hast set thy glory above the heavens. Out of the mouth of babes and sucklings hast thou ordained strength because of thine enemies, that thou mightest still the enemy and the avenger." Jesus quoted this verse of scripture and said, "Out of the mouth of babes and sucklings thou hast perfected praise" (Matthew 21:16). Strength and praise are the same according to the Word of God. God ordained praise to stop Satan in his tracks.

Once you have believed that you received because of the Word, your faith is in action. Through praise, you are throwing your faith up against that mountain of adversity in your life. Jesus said if you have faith and doubt not, you can speak to the mountain and it will be removed. You will have what you say. If you quit applying the force of faith, the mountain will not be removed. You want the mountain to keep moving until it sinks into the sea and is completely out of sight! Apply the force of faith by praising God that it is gone!

The only way Satan can stop you and your faith is through unbelief. He does not have power to stop God. He cannot stop that mountain from moving into the sea. The only way he can succeed is to make you quit applying the pressure.

The mountain may be sickness, disease, alcohol, family trouble, financial trouble or any evil work. Jesus bought and paid for the answer to all of it. You cannot face any problem that has not been taken care of through Calvary's Cross.

The psalmist David said, "I will praise thee, O Lord, with my whole heart; I will show forth all thy marvellous works. I will be glad and rejoice in thee: I will sing praise to thy name, O thou most High. When mine enemies are turned back, they shall fall and perish at thy presence" (Psalm 9:1-3). He did not say *if.* He said *when* the enemies fall back! As you praise God, those enemies will retreat. The Bible says He inhabits the praises of His people (Psalm 22:3).

Praise is not something you just feel once in a while. God is worthy of your praise. The Bible says to offer the sacrifice of praise. What did Israel do in the Old Testament when they had problems they could not overcome? The priest would offer sacrifices to God to bring Him on the scene and God would stop the onslaught of the enemy. As a new covenant believer, you are a priest of God. No other sacrifice can be offered. Jesus offered the ultimate blood sacrifice. As a priest, you offer the sacrifice of praise. Hebrews 13:15 says, "By him therefore let us offer the sacrifice of praise to God continually, that is, the fruit of our lips giving thanks to his name."

In Luke 17, Jesus ministered to 10 men who had leprosy. They said, "Jesus, Master, have mercy on us. And when he saw them, he said unto them, Go show yourselves unto the priests. And it came to pass, that, as they went, they were cleansed" (verses 13-14). Verse 15 says, "And one of them, when he saw that he was healed, turned back, and with a loud voice glorified [praised] God." They were all cleansed. But only one praised God unashamedly. Jesus said, "Were not the ten cleansed? but where are the nine?" Then He said to the man, "...Thy faith hath made thee whole" (verse 19). The others were cleansed but he was made whole! His faith kept working. His mountain did not stop at the seashore or sink halfway into the sea! No trace of his mountain was left. Whatever the disease had destroyed was restored.

That is the kind of power you can have right now in your own life. If you are not familiar with praising God, or it makes you feel uncomfortable, ask God to show you how. You can start by reading the Psalms aloud. They speak of the great and mighty works of God. They praise Him for His goodness, power and mercy. God is faithful to perfect your praises!

The Prayer of Committal

If you will practice what I am about to share with you, this will be the last day you will ever have a worried thought. You can commit yourself and all the cares and worries of your mind to Him and enjoy divine peace.

God is vehemently against worry. It does not produce anything but stress, strain and death. Jesus preached against it. Paul preached against it. The whole Bible is against worry because Satan designed it.

Take Philippians 4:6-7 as a command. "Be careful for nothing; but in every thing by prayer and supplication with thanksgiving let your requests be made known unto God. And the peace of God, which passeth all understanding, shall keep your hearts and minds through Christ Jesus." *The Amplified Bible* says, "Do not fret or have any anxiety about anything." First Peter 5:6-7 says, "Humble yourselves therefore under the mighty hand of God, that he may exalt you in due time. Casting *all* your care upon him...." Not 75 percent of your care. Not everything but your kids or everything but your finances. Your confession every morning should be, "I do not have a care, because it has been cast over on my Lord." Cast out every worried thought that would trample its way into your thinking. Roll it over onto Him.

For example let's say you were standing about 20 feet away from me and I tossed my car keys to you. If someone else were to come to me and say, "Brother Copeland, I need the keys to your car. I need to use it." I would say, "I can't help you. I cast my keys over on him. I don't have them." I didn't say those keys ceased to exist, nor that he could not have them. I didn't say I couldn't get them back. If I went to get them, you would give them back to me. But if someone wants the car keys, they will have to talk to you because I cast them over on you.

That's what we need to do with our cares. We must cast them over on the Lord and not take them back! If Satan brings a worried thought to your mind, saying, *What if...*, you can tell him to talk to God about it. It is in His hands, not yours!

Many people want God to supernaturally remove their worry. But that's not the way to get the peace of God. God's peace comes by acting on His Word that says to cast all of your worry and anxiety over on Him. You must replace those thoughts with the Word. Philippians 4:8 says to think on "whatsoever things are true...honest...just...lovely...of good report; if there be any virtue, and if there be any praise, think on these things."

You are the one who must control your mind. The Word says the peace of God will garrison and mount guard over your heart and mind (Philippians 4:7, *The Amplified Bible*). But you are going to have to do something. You must keep your thoughts under control.

Second Corinthians 10:5 says, "Casting down imaginations,

and every high thing that exalteth itself against the knowledge of God, and bringing into captivity every thought to the obedience of Christ." People have told me they can't quit worrying. They can! Anyone can stop worrying. The verse before that says the weapons of our warfare are not carnal, but powerful through God to the pulling down of strongholds. The strongholds of Satan are in the mind. He makes suggestions like, *It won't work this time,* and *What if...* and, *But....*

The power of God begins to operate when you cast your care over on Him. As long as you worry about it, you only hinder the flow of His power and tie His hands.

Meditate on these three scriptures: 1 Peter 5:6-7; 2 Corinthians 10:5 and Philippians 4:6. Joshua 1:8 says if you will meditate in the Word day and night, you will be able to see how to do it. Philippians 4:9 says, "Those things, which ye have both learned, and received, and heard, and seen in me, do...." As you give your attention to these scriptures, the Holy Spirit will reveal this truth to you and you will then be able to act on it!

Philippians 4:13 is the finale: "I can do all things through Christ which strengtheneth me." You don't have to worry again. The greater One dwells in you. He is able to put you over. Commit to it. You will never worry again.

Chapter 7
Fasting and Prayer

There are two categories of fasting: a proclaimed fast (Joel 1:14), and a personal fast as Jesus described in Matthew 6.

First, you do not fast to impress God. Some people think that if they fast long enough, it will influence Him to do something for them. Punishing yourself does not impress the Lord. It will only make you very, very hungry! Fasting changes you, not God.

Let's look at a proclaimed fast. Sometimes situations arise in which you need divine direction. A proclaimed fast brings believers into a place of hearing from God. When you find out how to pray about the situation, you can move in the same area of faith in one accord.

Second Chronicles 20:1-6 says:

> It came to pass after this also, that the children of Moab, and the children of Ammon, and with them other beside the Ammonites, came against Jehoshaphat to battle. Then there came some that told Jehoshaphat, saying, There cometh a great multitude against thee from beyond the sea on this side Syria; and, behold, they be in Hazazontamar, which is Engedi. And Jehoshaphat feared, and set himself to seek the Lord, and proclaimed a fast throughout all Judah.... And Jehoshaphat stood in the congregation of Judah and Jerusalem, in the house of the Lord, before the new court, and said, O Lord God of our fathers, art not thou God in heaven.... And in thine hand is there not power and might, so that none is able to withstand thee?

The main reason a proclaimed fast brings results is

because it directs people's minds toward God. They drop all other things and center their attention on Him. This brings His manifest presence in their midst.

While the believers in 2 Chronicles were in one accord, it says, "Then upon Jahaziel the son of Zechariah, the son of Benaiah, the son of Jeiel, the son of Mattaniah, a Levite of the sons of Asaph, came the spirit of the Lord in the midst of the congregation" (verse 14). Did you notice that the Spirit of God did not come on Jehoshaphat? He was the leader. Thank God someone in the congregation was sensitive to the Holy Spirit! "And he said, Hearken ye, all Judah, and ye inhabitants of Jerusalem, and thou king Jehoshaphat, Thus saith the Lord unto you, Be not afraid nor dismayed by reason of this great multitude; for the battle is not yours, but God's" (verse 15). Imagine how good that sounded to their ears! The Holy Ghost spoke. That is what they were seeking.

This principle will also work in our day. A New Testament example is found in Acts 13:1-2: "Now there were in the church that was at Antioch certain prophets and teachers.... As they ministered to the Lord, and fasted, the Holy Ghost said, Separate me Barnabas and Saul for the work whereunto I have called them." That assignment brought into being two-thirds of the New Testament. What an important day! Those men did not realize the magnitude of God's plan. They were simply being obedient.

The Holy Ghost spoke in the midst of a group of ordinary men who were fasting, praying and ministering to the Lord. This set into motion something that absolutely changed the world!

In that kind of atmosphere, God is given the opportunity to speak. A proclaimed fast is valuable and effective then, because it causes unity and singleness of purpose. It operates on the same principle as the prayer of agreement or united prayer—it produces power.

These believers received their instructions from God. They laid their hands on Saul and Barnabas and sent them forth. The results of their ministry were astounding!

By contrast, in Matthew 6:16-18, Jesus spoke of the personal fast. "Moreover when ye fast, be not, as the hypocrites, of a sad countenance: for they disfigure their faces, that they may appear unto men to fast. Verily I say unto you, They have their reward. But thou, when thou fastest, anoint thine head, and wash thy face; that thou appear not unto men to fast, but unto thy Father which is in secret: and thy Father, which seeth in secret, shall reward thee openly." Jesus really put the responsibility on you and me here. He did not say, *if* you fast, He said *when* you fast.

Rewards for personal fasting are on two different levels. One is from the admiration of men. They say, "Oh, can he fast! I wish I could do that. Don't you know he's spiritual." Jesus said not to be a hypocrite and look sad, making it obvious to men that you are fasting.

An open reward comes from God when you fast in secret. You can believe for this reward when you go into the fast. Be specific about its purpose. If you believe for the reward at the outset, the pressure from your physical body will lessen. Remembering the results, and the reward being obtained, makes fasting easier.

Fasting in the New Testament is not for chastisement. *Chastise* means "to instruct." "For whom the Lord loveth he chasteneth..." (Hebrews 12:6). He uses His Word to teach you.

New Testament and Old Testament repentance are two different things. Old Testament repentance meant to be sorry to the point of self-infliction or mourning. Under the New Covenant, the word *repentance* means "to completely turn around, to change your mind."

If you are a born-again Christian, God will not chastise

you through physical punishment. He will instruct you spiritually (Hebrews 12:9). Jesus said, "The words that I speak unto you, they are spirit, and they are life" (John 6:63). He will use His Word.

How did Peter move the men's hearts on the Day of Pentecost? With the words he preached. They were anointed, Holy Ghost-filled words that pricked their hearts. The Bible says the Word of God is good for reproof and correction (2 Timothy 3:16). In the literal Hebrew, Isaiah 53:5 says, "He bore our chastisement by punishment." You never, ever have to be punished by God. He deals with you through His Word!

Punishment is not in God's order of things for His family. He is available to lead and care for you. His desire is to abundantly supply your every need according to His riches in glory.

With these things in mind, let's study Isaiah 58. God explains the kind of fast to which He is calling the Body of Christ. He said, "Is not this the fast that I have chosen? to loose the bands of wickedness, to undo the heavy burdens, and to let the oppressed go free, and that ye break every yoke?" (verse 6).

We have been delivered from the power of darkness through the substitutionary sacrifice of Jesus. The price has been paid. If there is any oppressive yoke, the believer can and should be free from it. This is the fast that God has chosen: to loose the bands of wickedness, to undo the heavy burdens, to let the oppressed go free and to break *every* enslaving yoke. You can fast to set your whole congregation free of Satan's oppression. God calls us to fast to bring the spirit man into ascendancy over the flesh. This enhances intercession and sets the captives free!

There are also personal, spiritual rewards. Isaiah 58:8 says, "Then [when you have fasted] shall thy light break forth as the morning, and thine health shall spring forth speedily...."

What is the light of God? Psalm 119:130 says, "The entrance of thy words giveth light...." You begin to receive things from the light of God's Word. He will reveal His Word to you. When you have revelation knowledge of the Word you have confidence in it.

God told Joshua to meditate on the Word day and night so he would observe to do all that was written in it (Joshua 1:8). In other words, it will be revealed to you how to act on what is written in the Word.

He also said your health would spring forth speedily. Many Christians are not walking in divine health because they are ruled by the flesh. Fasting causes the spirit man to dominate the flesh. Faith for healing is easy when you are walking in the spirit.

Isaiah 58:8 in *The Amplified Bible* continues to say the glory of God will be your rear guard. The armor of God described in Ephesians 6 is all frontal.

Conditional to this fast is that all strife, talebearing and backbiting be purged. Every form of false, unkind or unjust speaking must be put away. The believer *must* operate in the love of God. Paul said, "Though I bestow all my goods to feed the poor...and have not charity, it profiteth me nothing" (1 Corinthians 13:3).

When the believer operates in the love of God, it prevents Satan from coming in and destroying the effectiveness of the fast. If you are not operating in love, your fasting will not profit you.

Fasting helps you to tune in to the spirit realm where healing—and all your inheritance—already belongs to you. Fasting will shut down the influences of the five physical senses so you can walk in the spirit. Your healing, victory, strength, faith and the power of God are all in the spirit. You fast so you can walk in the spirit and enjoy your inheritance.

This is what Jesus meant when the disciples came to Him and said, "Why could not we cast him [the devil] out?" (Mark 9:28). Jesus did not say, "Because you haven't fasted." He had said earlier, "Because of your unbelief" (Matthew 17:20). He had already given them the power to cast the devil out (Luke 10:19). They had been letting their flesh rule them. They were not fasting, praying and meditating on what Jesus had told them.

Jesus separated Himself to pray and fast regularly. He could minister to the people in faith. He stayed tapped in to His power source—the Holy Spirit. He lived in obedience to God. A fasted life, which is fasting and praying, spending time in the Word, and ministering to the Lord will keep you in a position to receive from God.

Take the time to get before God. Separate yourself from the things of the world, and fast. I am talking about fasting with rewards. Jesus said the Father would reward you.

Sometimes the only reward I seek in a fast is the deliverance of a friend, a situation that needs correcting, or God's anointing to minister more effectively. I fast and expect the anointing of God to operate.

A man living a fasted life lays things aside just to be with God. Once I fasted my newspaper. I had been spending anywhere from 15 minutes to an hour reading it each day. For one week I laid it aside to read the Word of God instead. Years have come and gone and I have not gone back to it. God honored that fast.

If you really want to enjoy life and break completely out of the ordinary, begin to live the high life of which Jesus spoke. He said if you will lose your life for His sake, you'll find it (Matthew 10:39). The Greek text says, "If you'll give up that low life, you will find the high life." This is one of the ways you shed the low life. The high life in the realm of the spirit is more than exciting! It is not just a religion full of "dos" and "don'ts."

As you begin to live the fasted life, the power in the spirit will begin to work for you. You will be building your foundation on God. A fasted life is one that feeds on the Word of God all the time and separates itself to God. It is a life consecrated and dedicated to Him.

Here is a five-step checklist for fasting. Put yourself in a position to receive from God spiritually. You can take these steps and order your thinking by them:

1. Decide the purpose of the fast.

2. Proclaim the fast before the Lord.

3. Believe you receive the reward (Matthew 6:18)—before the fast. The reward will probably be related to the first step. The purpose of the fast will have a great deal to do with the rewards involved. If you are fasting for revelation knowledge, the reward would be receiving the knowledge you desire.

4. Minister to the Lord. "Let the word of Christ dwell in you richly in all wisdom; teaching and admonishing one another in psalms and hymns and spiritual songs, singing with grace in your hearts to the Lord" (Colossians 3:16). One of the best things you can do to learn how to minister to the Lord is to read the Psalms. You minister to the Lord by speaking of His mighty works. When you begin to praise and minister to Him, He will get involved with you! You need to fellowship with Him and He needs to hear praise and thanksgiving. I heard myself saying to the Lord one day, "Jesus, You are my High Priest. Take my praise and minister it unto my Father. Make it a sweet incense to His nostrils. Blot out all the sin that

has come up before Him from this miserable planet. Minister my praise and love and adoration to Him. Cause it to be just what He needs today. I want to bless His heart. I do not want Him to be grieved by the sinfulness of man." I began to realize that my heavenly Father needs this. Earthly fathers long to hear their children tell them how much they love them instead of just begging for things. "I love you, Dad," is a statement that captures a father's heart. Just think how much that means to our heavenly Father!

5. Minister to others. Always minister to others after the fast. You need to use the spiritual power within you to meet the needs of people. If you fast according to the Word of God, you will be spiritually built up. Minister to others during the fast only as you are led of the Father.

Living the fasted life will cause you to produce the fruit of the spirit. This fruit comes forth from the reborn human spirit. The Holy Spirit is certainly all these things, but He is not in you to bear fruit. He is in you to teach you how to bear fruit. He is your teacher, your intercessor, your standby and helper. He gives you the power—you bear the fruit.

Galatians 5:22-23 says, "But the fruit of the Spirit is love, joy, peace, longsuffering [patience], gentleness, goodness, faith, meekness, temperance: against such there is no law." These are spiritual forces. Proverbs 4:20-23 says, "My son, attend to my words; incline thine ear unto my sayings. Let them not depart from thine eyes; keep them in the midst of thine heart. For they are life unto those that find them, and health to all their flesh. Keep thy heart with all diligence; for out of it are the issues of life." One translation says, "Out of it [the heart] flow the forces of life." Not one force in this list will produce death.

Love produces life. Joy is a life-giving force, etc.

Fasting shuts down the influence of the body, so the spirit man can dominate. As you stay in the Word and in fellowship with God, you will not be flesh-ruled, you will glorify God in your body.

Chapter 8
Hindrances to Prayer

God's desire is to answer every prayer. He has even given us His Word so we can pray according to His will. Unanswered prayer is not the result of God's unwillingness to use His power, but because of hindrances we allow to overcome us. The Bible says His eyes look to and fro throughout the earth to show Himself strong in behalf of those whose hearts are perfect toward Him (2 Chronicles 16:9). When we are aware of these hindrances and how to avoid them, we will experience the joy of answered prayer.

Jesus said in Matthew 21:22, "And all things, whatsoever ye shall ask in prayer, believing, ye shall receive." He did not say that a few things you pray for would come to pass, or that just a prayer now and then would be answered. Jesus said, "And *all* things, whatsoever ye shall ask in prayer, believing...." He said *believing*. Then, "...ye shall receive."

Doubt and Unbelief

Two of the greatest hindrances to the believer's prayer life are doubt and unbelief. Though similar, there are differences. Doubt is the thief of God's greater blessings. It keeps a man in a state of separation from Him. Some men doubt there is a God or doubt He will perform His Word in response to their prayers. As a result, they do not respond to His Word. This hinders His power in their behalf.

Doubt comes from ignorance of God's Word. For example, many have the idea that God will no longer heal or they think He is not interested in their financial affairs. Consequently, their prayers are hindered.

God has given us His Word to keep our minds renewed. It

is through the knowledge of His Word that we can fellowship with Him, find out His will and act accordingly. For instance, a man determines that it is God's will to heal him. When he prays according to God's Word, he can be sure God will move in his behalf. The knowledge of God's Word expels the force of doubt.

Unbelief is when a man knows there is a God, yet does not believe His Word. He knows what the Bible says, but he has chosen to believe what he can see and feel instead. This will definitely hinder his prayer life.

In order to expel doubt and unbelief, you must make God's Word final authority in every matter, not allowing religious tradition, or what you think about the situation, to be the deciding factor. Pray according to the will of God and believe you receive when you pray. God's Word is His will. He does not will one thing and say another. God cannot lie. Refuse to be moved by anything except what God's Word tells you.

When you pray, expect things to change. God's Word will not fail.

Lack of Knowledge of Our Right-Standing With God

The second great hindrance to prayer is the lack of knowledge of our right-standing with God. Most people do not understand what God actually did in Christ Jesus at Calvary. Jesus became our sin so we could become the righteousness of God (2 Corinthians 5:21). Righteousness is right-standing with God. Your righteousness is vitally important in the field of prayer. We saw in Ephesians 6 that righteousness is a breastplate.

Your right-standing with God gives you the right to approach God in prayer without a sense of guilt, sin or condemnation. There is a confidence you experience, knowing you will receive when you ask in faith, believing.

Romans 3:21-23 says, "But now the righteousness of God

without the law is manifested, being witnessed by the law and the prophets; even the righteousness of God which is by faith of Jesus Christ unto all and upon all them that believe: for there is no difference: for all have sinned, and come short of the glory of God." The Apostle Paul said the right to expect God to answer your prayers is upon all and unto all them that believe. No man on earth deserves God's righteousness. But when he receives Jesus as Lord, he is placed in right-standing with God. He is made the righteousness of God by grace through faith.

The Word says God is not holding sin against the world (2 Corinthians 5:17-21). He sent Jesus to take your place. If you recognize this and let Him be your righteousness, God will answer your prayer as if Jesus Himself prayed it. When you realize that, you have your breastplate of righteousness working for you. Something priceless is working in your life.

You may think you are the worst sinner the world has ever seen. Any man who considers himself so far gone God cannot reach him, must think that he is bigger than God. Through the new birth, Jesus has made us the righteousness of God through His sacrifice at Calvary. No sin Satan could dream up is big enough to change that!

Romans 5:17 says, "For if by one man's offence death reigned by one...." (That, of course, was the offense committed by Adam in the Garden of Eden. It brought death into the earth.) "...much more they which receive abundance of grace and of the gift of righteousness shall reign in life by one, Jesus Christ." As born-again believers, we have been made the righteousness of God in Christ. Therefore, we have been given the ability to reign in this life. We must take advantage of our right-standing relationship with God. We will then see the results we desire in prayer.

James 5:16 says, "...The effectual fervent prayer of a righteous man availeth much." You may have read that verse of

scripture and thought, *You know, if I were just righteous....*
Jesus died for you! The righteousness He bought for you at
Calvary is more than enough to make your prayers effective.
Romans 5:17 says righteousness is a gift and Romans 3:22
says it is "unto all...them that believe."

God is moved when a man believes His Word. If you are
believing, then James 5:16 says your prayer *will* avail much.
Faith qualifies you for answered prayer!

You have a God-given right to expect God to answer your
prayer. Don't let the devil deceive you into thinking God will
not answer. Jesus said whatsoever you shall ask the Father
in His Name, He will give it to you. As long as you can pray,
believing, you will not be defeated. If you know your right-
standing with God, you will not be overcome.

Ignorance of Our Right to Use the Name of Jesus

Lack of knowledge of our right to use the Name of Jesus is
the third great hindrance to prayer. A great void of knowledge
of the power in Jesus' Name exists in most Christian circles.
John 16:23 says, "And in that day ye shall ask me nothing.
Verily, verily, I say unto you, Whatsoever ye shall ask the
Father in my name, he will give it you."

Go before the Father in Jesus' Name. You are already
going before Him in Jesus' power and His faith. Your prayer
will be answered.

No believer would ever doubt the *power* of Jesus' Name
or that the Father hears that Name in prayer. What, then, is
the problem? The root of unbelief where the Name of Jesus is
concerned is in not believing we have the right to use it. Will
the Father hear me pray in that Name?

I have a right to use my name because it was given to me
by my father. He gave me the name of Kenneth Copeland. I

came into the world with the right to use it. When you make Jesus Christ the Lord of your life, God becomes your Father. The Bible says any man who believes that Jesus is the Christ, is born of God (1 John 5:1). Once you realize you have the right to use the family name, you will see God's power operating mightily in your behalf.

Gloria and I were driving down the freeway one day. The car in front of us began to fishtail. The second time it came across the freeway, it hit the curb and started up on its side. Gloria shouted at the top of her voice, "Jesus, help them!" It was so strong when she shouted the Name of Jesus that the car slammed back down on all four wheels and straightened out, coming to a full stop. God responds to the Name of Jesus!

I believe Satan and his cohorts are reminded of their defeat at Calvary every time they hear the Name of Jesus!

You should become so aware of the power in that Name that you guard it like your own—because it is yours!

Unforgiveness and Strife

Another hindrance to prayer is found in Mark 11:25-26. It says, "And when ye stand praying, forgive, if ye have aught against any: that your Father also which is in heaven may forgive you your trespasses. But if ye do not forgive, neither will your Father which is in heaven forgive your trespasses." This is vital. Prayer will not work without forgiveness. I cannot overemphasize its importance. Jesus prayed, "Our Father which art in heaven, Hallowed be thy name. Thy kingdom come. Thy will be done, as in heaven, so in earth. Give us day by day our daily bread. And forgive us our sins; for we also forgive every one that is indebted to us. And lead us not into temptation; but deliver us from evil" (Luke 11:2-4). Spiritual principles are involved here. You can keep these hindrances from stopping the results of your prayers. Harmony makes the prayer system work.

This attitude of forgiveness begins at home. Jesus said if any two of you will agree on earth, He will be in your midst. A man and his wife should be the strongest agreement force there is. Satan goes to great lengths to separate a man from his wife and family. He wants them out of agreement.

First Peter 3:7 says, "Likewise, ye husbands, dwell with them [your wives] according to knowledge [according to the Word of God], giving honour unto the wife, as unto the weaker vessel, and as being heirs together of the grace of life; that your prayers be not hindered." If a husband is not honoring his wife as he should, his prayers are hindered. The burden of harmony is not on the wife. The husband is the authority in his household. The power of God is available to the man and wife who purpose to stay in harmony.

As you come against unforgiveness and reach for harmony, you will experience Jesus in your midst! He said, "If a man love me, he will keep my words: and my Father will love him, and we will come unto him, and make our abode with him" (John 14:23).

You cannot say you are pleasing God and hold something against someone. First John 4:20 says, "If a man say, I love God, and hateth his brother, he is a liar: for he that loveth not his brother whom he hath seen, how can he love God whom he hath not seen?" This includes family members as well.

Strife and unforgiveness hinder your prayer life. Strife is merely acting on unforgiveness. James 3:16 says, "For where envying and strife is, there is confusion and every evil work." When you take confusion and add it to Satan's work, problems arise. You will have a disaster in the making. Jesus is not in the midst of that. Determine you are not going to respond in strife. The next time someone says something rude, unmannerly or unkind to you, or about someone else, make the decision not to join in. Don't carry strife any further.

Second Timothy 2:24-26 says that because of strife, Satan can capture Christians at his will. Jesus said the thief comes to steal, kill and destroy (John 10:10). That is the only reason he gets involved in your life. The believer belongs to God and has every right to walk free, but wholeness—spirit, soul, body, financially and socially—is only achieved through peace and harmony.

The absence of strife is the key to getting rid of confusion and evil. It is the predominant, primary prerequisite for answered prayer. Stop Satan from working in your life. You do not want him in your home or your prayer life. So the first thing to do is begin to forgive. Get strife out of your life. Jesus said to ask and you will receive, that your joy may be made full. Your joy will be strong.

Matthew 18:19-20 will not work just because two people say the same thing. The prayer of agreement is effective because of its motivating force—love!

As you read this, take the opportunity right now to rid yourself of strife, disharmony or unforgiveness. Confess it. Jesus is faithful to forgive you (1 John 1:9). Give God the opportunity to create a system of harmony around you and your prayer life will begin to work.

Lack of Knowledge of Fellowship

Lack of knowledge of the value of fellowshiping with God will also hinder your prayer life. If you do not know the importance of close, intimate fellowship with God, you will not likely see results in prayer. Set apart a specific time to be alone with Him and to direct all your attention toward Him. It is easy to say, "I don't have time to stop everything else, so I'll just fellowship with God 'on the go.' If He has something to tell me, He can say it while I'm doing this or that." Yes, you can commune with God wherever you are and in whatever you are doing, but you must get quiet and spend quality time in His presence to hear His voice. When you are "on the go," you will do most of the talking.

The Bible says in 1 John 1:3-4, "That which we have seen and heard declare we unto you, that ye also may have fellowship with us: and truly our fellowship is with the Father, and with his Son Jesus Christ. And these things write we unto you, that your joy may be full." You are called into fellowship with the Father. This is why God made man in the first place—to fellowship with Him.

The Bible says we have been given in our spirit a cry that says, "Abba, Father." Scholars tell us the closest English word we have to *abba* is "daddy." Our relationship with Him has all the freedom of "Daddy," and yet the reverence and respect of "Father." You can fellowship with God on both levels, as your Daddy and as your Father.

Fellowshiping with the Father gives Him the opportunity to reveal His Word to you by His Spirit. Fellowship brings joy to your relationship. Jesus said, "...your joy no man taketh from you" (John 16:22). That joy is your strength.

The Word of God brings faith. Fellowship will cause it to become effective. Fellowship will drive out all fear and doubt. It brings you into a love relationship with the Father and love casts out fear. Through intimate fellowship, God will personally reveal His love to you.

Fellowship with the Father because you desire His company, not out of a lack of faith. Do it because you love God and He loves you. Your relationship is founded on love instead of obligation when you choose to fellowship with God.

God and His Word are one. So when you fellowship with Him through His Word, He responds to you by His Spirit. Learn to fellowship with God. Do it by faith and expect Him to respond. Say, "Father, I didn't come to beg You for anything. I came to visit with You. You have things to tell me and I'm going to be quiet and just listen. I want to hear from You. Most of all, I just want to be with You, in Your presence. I want to watch You run the universe. I want Your slightest whim to be my command."

The first time I did that, the Lord spoke to me and said, *Son, you don't know how that thrills the heart of a Father.* I heard Him speak to me in words you hear when you talk with a friend. I heard it in my heart as if it were an audible voice. Psalm 16:11 says fullness of joy is in His presence. What joy it brought!

He enjoys our fellowship, too. It brings Him fulfillment and joy as well. The greatest times you will ever have are times spent fellowshiping with God!

Chapter 9
A Deeper Life in Prayer

To summarize, I want to share some necessary guidelines in the development of a deeper life in prayer. These will cause your prayer life to become accurate.

Scriptural principles of prayer will bring about an accurate prayer life. Accuracy produces results. Charles Finney wrote in one of his memorandums: "I have had some experiences in prayer of late that have alarmed me." I thought about that for a while. I realized I hadn't really had any prayer experiences that were "alarming." I made the decision to get involved in my prayer life like he did. As my prayer life deepened, I began to have some awesome experiences.

When you are accurate in your prayer life, you are operating out of your spirit rather than just your mind. Your spiritual ears are open to the voice of God. Train yourself not to make a move without listening to the Spirit of God. He is the intercessor. You are the mouthpiece. "Likewise the Spirit also helpeth our infirmities: for we know not what we should pray for as we ought: but the Spirit itself maketh intercession for us with groanings which cannot be uttered" (Romans 8:26). If you never attempt to be accurate in prayer, you will never be sure about the results. You'll just be hoping for something to happen.

The coming of the Holy Spirit changed the whole perspective of prayer. This is a key to accuracy. Jesus said,

And in that day [after the Holy Spirit comes] ye shall ask me nothing. Verily, verily, I say unto you, Whatsoever ye shall ask the Father in my name, he will give it you. Hitherto have ye asked nothing in my name: ask, and ye shall receive, that your joy may be full. These things have I spoken unto you in proverbs:

but the time cometh, when I shall no more speak unto you in proverbs, but I shall show you plainly of the Father. At that day ye shall ask in my name: and I say not unto you, that I will pray the Father for you: for the Father himself loveth you, because ye have loved me, and have believed that I came out from God (John 16:23-27).

Pray to the Father in Jesus' Name. Jesus endorses your prayer. With His Name, you are given free access to the throne of God. You short-circuit the system when you make your requests to Jesus. He said to pray this way: "Our Father which art in heaven, Hallowed be thy name..." (Luke 11:2). If you want Jesus to endorse your prayer, you need to pray to the Father in His Name.

Believe you receive when you pray. Mark 11:24 states, "Therefore I say unto you, What things soever ye desire, when ye pray, believe that ye receive them, and ye shall have them." *The Amplified Bible* says, "For this reason I am telling you, whatever you ask for in prayer, believe (trust and be confident) that it is granted to you, and you will [get it]." Note the word *granted.* John 16:23 in *The Amplified Bible* says, "And when that time comes, you will ask nothing of Me [you will need to ask Me no questions]. I assure you, most solemnly I tell you, that My Father will grant you whatever you ask in My Name...." *To grant* means "to bestow possession of by title or deed." You need no other evidence than God's Word. Believe you receive. Learn to do this every time you pray and learn to pray with your Bible open. Don't major on the problem. Start with the answer. Be specific when you pray. God said He would watch over His Word to perform it (Jeremiah 1:12). Once you are involved in His Word, He can work for you. Be fully persuaded that God can perform His Word for you (Romans 4:21).

Forgive. Your faith will not work accurately in an unforgiving heart. Jesus commanded us to forgive (Mark 11:24-25). Your prayers will not work effectively with sin in your life. The promises don't work without meeting the conditions. All you have to do is confess unforgiveness. He is faithful and just to forgive you and cleanse you from all unrighteousness. Keep your prayer life exact by keeping sin out of your life. Keep the forgiveness door to your heart open. Maintain fellowship with your Father.

Depend on the Holy Spirit in your prayer life. Romans 8:26 says: "Likewise the Spirit also helpeth our infirmities: for we know not what we should pray for as we ought: but the Spirit itself maketh intercession for us with groanings which cannot be uttered." The Holy Spirit is your helper, standby, teacher, strengthener, comforter, intercessor, counselor. Depend on Him when you pray. Operate in faith instead of by feeling.

Allow the spirit realm to become a reality to you. Purpose to see beyond the realm of your five physical senses. Remember, you are a spirit. You have a soul. You live in a body. Your body is just the "earth suit" for your spirit. It is not the real you.

Many people want to see visions or an angel appear. Seeking after something you can see with your natural eye or hear with your natural ear is the lowest form of spiritual manifestation. If you are not in tune with God spiritually, you would not be able to understand a vision if you saw one. When you become spiritually in tune, you do not need any confirmation from your senses. The Word is enough evidence. God will confirm His Word to you when you are in faith (Mark 16:20). Rely on the Holy Spirit.

Learn to pray for others. First Timothy 2:1 says, "I exhort therefore, that, first of all, supplications, prayers, intercessions, and giving of thanks, be made for all men." Train yourself to do this first of all. The result of praying for others is that you live a quiet and peaceable life in all godliness and honesty. Anytime the Church of Jesus Christ is in turmoil, its members are not praying for others.

The Apostle Paul said spiritual maturity demands each believer does his part (Ephesians 4:15-16). Verse 16 says, "From whom the whole body fitly joined together and compacted by that which every joint supplieth, according to the effectual working in the measure of every part, maketh increase of the body unto the edifying of itself in love." Each part has a contribution to make to the rest of the Body. We are to supply to one another as we draw from God through our fellowship with Him.

As you become involved with intercessory prayer for the Body of Christ, the whole operation will begin to be successful. When you pray and supply the things that cause the Body to be compacted together, Satan cannot tear it down. Pray the prayer of intercession. It will cause us to come together in unity.

I suggest you set up a time and a place to pray the prayer of intercession. Even if it is just for five minutes. It will grow into 10 minutes, 15 minutes, 20 minutes and so on. Your intercession has a positive effect on the lives of others.

Spend time praying in the spirit. Jude 20 says, "But ye, beloved, building up yourselves on your most holy faith, praying in the Holy Ghost." Take the time to pray daily in other tongues specifically for edification. It will draw you into a deeper life in prayer and will keep you prepared at all times. First Corinthians 14:4 says, "He that speaketh in an unknown tongue edifieth himself." The word *edify* translated in the Greek means the same as "charging a battery."

Praying in other tongues will keep you tuned in to the Spirit. It will help you to overcome the weakness of your flesh.

God needs a Church that is not walking after the flesh. As we walk in the spirit and sow to the spirit, we stay "charged" and ready to do battle in the spirit! God needs each one of us in this critical time.

Always base your prayer on the Word of God. Prayer based on the Word is based on God's will. God's Word is His will. James 4:3 says, "Ye ask, and receive not, because ye ask amiss...." If you pray according to God's Word, you cannot ask amiss. All Scripture is profitable for correction and instruction" (2 Timothy 3:16). When you pray in line with God's Word, you can have the confidence that your prayers are free from error.

Chapter 10
Prayers

Putting Prayer to Work!

Prayer based on the Word is already in line with the will of God. First John 5:14-15 tells us that we know God hears us and answers our prayer when we ask according to His will. The following prayers have been compiled from the Word of God on various subjects. They will aid you in getting your personal prayer life off to a good start.

I have included some very brief instruction for making Jesus your Lord and for receiving the Baptism in the Holy Spirit. Of course, there is much more but these will get you started. God will honor your prayers and give you direction.

Some of these prayers are confessions of the Word of God, not petitions. Psalm 103:20 says, "Bless the Lord, ye his angels, that excel in strength, that do his commandments, hearkening unto the voice of his word." The angels hearken or listen to God's Word and cooperate with Him in bringing it to pass in your behalf. God is alert and active, watching over His Word to perform it (Jeremiah 1:12). The speaking or confessing of the Word by the believer activates the power of God. He has said, "So shall My word be that goes forth out of My mouth: it shall not return to Me void [without producing any effect, useless], but it shall accomplish that which I please and purpose, and it shall prosper in the thing for which I sent it" (Isaiah 55:11, *The Amplified Bible*). As you speak God's Word over situations and circumstances, it will produce a positive effect and prosper in those areas.

Scriptures used in the following prayers and confessions are taken from the *King James Version* and *The Amplified Bible.*

To Make Jesus the Lord of Your Life

Do you know where you stand with God?

If you have never made Jesus the Lord of your life, then you are separated from God through sin. You are the reason God sent Jesus to the cross. John 3:16 says, "For God so loved the world, that he gave his only begotten Son, that whosoever believeth in him should not perish, but have everlasting life." God loved you so much He gave His only begotten Son for you.

Second Corinthians 5:21 says God made Jesus, who knew no sin, to be sin for us. Jesus is the spotless Son of God. He knew no sin, but God made Him to be sin for us. Sin was the reason Jesus came to earth. He died on the Cross and went to hell for one reason: to pay the price for sin. Once that price was paid, Jesus was raised from the dead, triumphant over Satan, and the sin problem was taken care of.

God is not holding your sin against you. He sent Jesus as your substitute. He paid the debt. Now you can receive the credit for what He did in your place (Isaiah 53:3-5).

The price has been paid, but it's not an automatic thing. You must choose to accept what He did for you and receive Him as your personal Savior. If you have never done so, choose Him now. Repent of your sin (turn totally from it) and pray this prayer. When you do, the power of God will make you a new creature in Christ Jesus. Say:

Heavenly Father, in the Name of Jesus, I present myself to You. I pray and ask Jesus to be Lord over my life. I believe it in my heart, so I say it with my mouth: Jesus has been raised from the dead. This moment, I make Him the Lord over my life. Jesus, come into my heart. I believe this moment that I am saved. I say it now: I am reborn. I am a Christian. I am a child of Almighty God.

Scripture References: John 1:12, 3:16, 6:37, 10:10, 14:6, 16:8-9; Romans 3:23, 5:8, 10:9-10, 13; 2 Corinthians 5:17, 19, 21.

To Be Filled With the Holy Spirit

After Jesus Christ was raised from the dead and before He ascended into heaven, He left us this promise: "Ye shall receive power, after that the Holy Ghost is come upon you: and ye shall be witnesses unto me...[throughout] the earth" (Acts 1:8). The Holy Spirit is the One who endues us with power for our Christian walk and to do the works of Jesus (John 14:12).

God has already sent the Holy Spirit. He came to earth on the Day of Pentecost (Acts 2). Now it is up to you to receive Him into your life.

Once you are born again, you can receive the Holy Spirit just as you received Jesus—by faith in God's Word. All you must do is ask Him. Jesus said, "If ye then, being evil, know how to give good gifts unto your children: how much more shall your heavenly Father give the Holy Spirit to them that *ask* him?" (Luke 11:13). The Holy Spirit will empower you with God's own power! You need His power working in you—ask Him now.

My heavenly Father, I am a believer. I am Your child and You are my Father. Jesus is my Lord. I believe with all my heart that Your Word is true. Your Word says that, if I will ask, I will receive the Holy Spirit, so in the Name of Jesus Christ my Lord, I am asking You to fill me to overflowing with Your precious Holy Spirit. Baptize me in the Holy Spirit. Because of Your Word, I believe that I now receive and I thank You for it. I believe that the Holy Spirit is within me and, by faith, I accept it. Now, Holy Spirit, rise up within me as I praise my God. I fully expect to speak with other tongues as You give me the utterance.

Meditate on these scriptures about the Holy Spirit: Luke 11:9-13; John 14:10, 12, 16-17; Acts 1:8, 2:4, 32-33, 38-39, 8:12-17, 10:44-46, 19:2, 5-6; 1 Corinthians 14:2-15, 18, 27; Ephesians 6:18; Jude 20.

A Prayer for Salvation in Behalf of Others

Father, I come before You in prayer and in faith, believing. Your Word says You desire all men to be saved and come into the knowledge of the truth, so I bring _____ before You this day.

I break the power of Satan from his assignments and activities in _____'s life in the Name of Jesus. Now, while Satan is bound, I ask that You send forth the perfect laborers to share the good news of the gospel in such a way that he/she will listen and understand it. As the truth is ministered, I believe _____ will come to his/her senses and come out of the snare of the devil and make Jesus the Lord of his/her life.

Father, I ask that You fill _____ with the knowledge of Your will in all wisdom and spiritual understanding. As I intercede in his/her behalf, I believe that the power of the Holy Spirit is activated and from this moment on, I shall praise and thank You for _____'s salvation.

I am confident that You are alert and active, watching over Your Word to perform it. It will not return to You void. It will accomplish that which You please, and prosper in the thing whereto it was sent. Therefore, my confession of faith is, "God has begun a good work in _____'s life and He will perform it and bring it to full completion until the day of Jesus Christ. In Jesus' Name. Amen.

Scripture References from *The Amplified Bible:* 2 Peter 3:9; Matthew 18:18, 9:37-38; 2 Timothy 2:26; Jeremiah 1:12; Isaiah 55:11; Philippians 1:6.

A Prayer for Health and Healing

Father, in the Name of Jesus, I confess Your Word concerning healing. I believe and say that Your Word will not return to You void, but will accomplish what it says it will. Therefore, I believe in the Name of Jesus, that I am healed according to 1 Peter 2:24. It is written in Your Word that Jesus Himself took my infirmities and bore my sicknesses (Matthew 8:17). Therefore, with great boldness and confidence, I say on the authority of that written Word that I am redeemed from the curse of sickness and I refuse to tolerate its symptoms.

Satan, I speak to you in the Name of Jesus and say that your principalities, powers, master spirits who rule the present darkness and your spiritual wickedness in heavenly places are bound from operating against me in any way. I am loosed from your assignment. I am the property of Almighty God and give you no place in me. I dwell in the secret place of the Most High God. I abide, remain stable and fixed, under the shadow of the Almighty, whose power no foe can withstand.

Now, Father, because I reverence and worship You, I have the assurance of Your Word that the angel of the Lord encamps around about me and delivers me from every evil work. No evil shall befall me, no plague or calamity shall come near my dwelling. I confess the Word of God abides in me and delivers to me perfect soundness of mind and wholeness in body and spirit from the deepest parts of my nature in my immortal spirit, even to the joints and marrow of my bones. That Word is medication and life to my flesh, for the law of the Spirit of life operates in me and makes me free from the law of sin and death.

I have on the whole armor of God. The shield of faith protects me from all the fiery darts of the wicked. Jesus is the High Priest of my confession, and I hold fast to my confession of faith in God's Word. I stand immovable and fixed in full assurance that I have health and healing *now* in the Name of Jesus.

Scripture References: Isaiah 55:11; Galatians 3:13; Ephesians 6:12; 2 Corinthians 10:4; James 4:7; Psalms 91:1, 34:7, 91:10; Hebrews 4:12, *The Amplified Bible;* Proverbs 4:20-22; Romans 8:2; Ephesians 6:16; Hebrews 4:14; Psalm 112:7.

A Prayer for a Harmonious Marriage

Father, in the Name of Jesus, it is written in Your Word that love is shed abroad in our hearts by the Holy Ghost who is given to us. Because You are in us, we acknowledge that love reigns supreme.

We believe that love is displayed in full expression, enfolding and knitting us together in truth, making us perfect for every good work to do Your will and working in us that which is well-pleasing in Your sight.

We desire to live and conduct ourselves and our marriage honorably and becomingly. We esteem it as precious, worthy and of great price. We commit ourselves to live in mutual harmony and accord with one another, delighting in each other, being of the same mind and united in spirit.

Father, we believe and say that we are gentle, compassionate, courteous, tenderhearted and humble-minded. We seek peace and it keeps our hearts in quietness and assurance. Because we follow after love and dwell in peace, our prayers are not hindered in any way in the Name of Jesus. We are heirs together of the grace of life.

We purpose together to live in agreement, to live in harmony, to live in peace, to live in power toward each other and toward all men. We confess that our marriage grows stronger day by day in the bond of unity because it is founded on Your Word and rooted and grounded in Your love. Father, we thank You for the performance of it in Jesus' Name.

Scripture References from *The Amplified Bible:* Romans 5:5; Philippians 1:9; Colossians 3:14, 1:10; Philippians 2:13, 2:2; Ephesians 4:32; Isaiah 32:17; Philippians 4:7; 1 Peter 3:7; Ephesians 3:17-18; Jeremiah 1:12.

A Prayer for Your Children

Father, Your Word is true and I believe it. Therefore, in the Name of Jesus, I believe in my heart and say with my mouth that Your Word prevails over my children. Your Word says You will pour out Your Spirit upon my offspring, and Your blessing upon my descendants. I believe and say that my children are wise, they take heed to and are the fruit of godly instruction and correction. I love my children and I will diligently discipline them early. Because of that, they give me delight and rest.

Father, I take Your Word that says You contend with him who contends with me and You give safety to my children and ease them day by day. I confess that You, Lord, give Your angels special charge over my children to accompany and defend and preserve them. I believe they find favor, good understanding and high esteem in Your sight, Lord, and in the sight of man.

I confess that my children are disciples, taught of You, Lord, and obedient to Your will. Great is their peace and undisturbed composure. I believe I receive wisdom and counsel in bringing up my children in Your discipline and instruction. Your Word declares that when they are old they will not depart from it. So, I commit them into Your keeping and I know, and have confident trust, that they are watched over and blessed of You all the days of their lives, in Jesus' Name.

Scripture References from *The Amplified Bible:* Mark 11:23; Isaiah 44:3; Proverbs 13:1, 24, 29:17; Isaiah 49:25; Psalm 91:11; Proverbs 3:4; Isaiah 54:13; Proverbs 2:6; Ephesians 6:4; Proverbs 22:6; Deuteronomy 28:6. Also see Deuteronomy 28:13; Psalm 127:3-5; Isaiah 55:11; Jeremiah 1:12, not included in prayer.

A Prayer for Our Government

Father, in Jesus' Name, I give thanks for our country and its government. I hold up in prayer before You the men and women in positions of authority. I pray for all people in authority over us in any way. I pray that the Spirit of the Lord rests upon them.

I believe that skillful and godly wisdom has entered into the hearts of our leaders and knowledge is pleasant to them. Discretion watches over them; understanding keeps them and delivers them from the way of evil and from evil men.

Your Word declares that "blessed is the nation whose God is the Lord." I receive Your blessing and declare with my mouth that Your people dwell safely in this land and that they prosper abundantly.

It is written in Your Word that the heart of the king is in the hand of the Lord and that You turn it whichever way You desire. I believe the heart of our leader is in Your hand and that his decisions are divinely directed of You.

I give thanks unto You that the good news of the gospel is published in our land. The Word of the Lord prevails and grows mightily in the hearts and lives of the people. I give thanks for this land and the leaders You have given to us, in Jesus' Name.

I proclaim that Jesus is Lord over my country.

Scripture References: 1 Timothy 2:1-2; Proverbs 2:11-12; *The Amplified Bible:* Psalm 33:12; Proverbs 21:1. Also see Jeremiah 1:12, not included in prayer.

To Walk in the Perfect Peace of God

Father, in Jesus' Name, I thank You that Your peace is my covenant right in Christ Jesus. I will keep my mind fixed on You, trust in You, and You will keep me in perfect peace.

I will not fret or have anxiety about anything, but in every circumstance and in everything by prayer and petition with thanksgiving, I will continue to make my wants known to You, Father. And Your peace, which transcends all understanding, shall garrison and mount guard over my mind and heart in Christ Jesus. I fix my mind only on that which is true, worthy of reverence, honorable, just, pure, lovely, kind and gracious. If there is anything worthy of praise, I will think on and weigh and take account only of these things.

I will let Your peace rule in my heart. As I do, I believe my calm and undisturbed heart and mind are life and health to my physical body. I humble myself under Your mighty hand, casting all of my concerns and anxieties on You once and for all, because I know You care for me affectionately.

I thank You, Father, that You have not given me a spirit of

timidity, of cowardice, of craven and cringing and fawning fear. The spirit I have from You is the spirit of power, love, a calm and well-balanced mind, and of discipline and self-control. You, Lord, are on my side. I will not fear. What can man do to me? You are my light and my salvation. Whom shall I fear or dread? You, Lord, are the refuge and stronghold of my life; of whom shall I be afraid? I love Your law, O Lord. Nothing shall offend me or make me stumble. I walk in great peace, in Jesus' Name, Amen.

Scripture References: Isaiah 26:3; *The Amplified Bible:* Philippians 4:6-8; Colossians 3:15; Proverbs 14:30; 1 Peter 5:6-7; 2 Timothy 1:7; Psalms 27:1, 118:6, 119:165.

Walking in the Wisdom and Guidance of the Holy Spirit

Father, in the Name of Jesus, I realize that as a believer, my body is the temple of the Holy Spirit. My acknowledgment of Your presence on a daily basis makes my faith in You effectual. I believe that You, heavenly Father, are leading me and guiding me by the Holy Spirit through my spirit, and illuminating my mind.

As I yield to the Holy Spirit, I believe that my steps are ordered of the Lord. I commit and trust myself wholly to His guidance, expecting Him to cause my thoughts to become agreeable to His will, so my plans will be established and succeed. I trust in the Lord with all my heart and lean not on my own understanding. As I acknowledge Him, He directs me in paths of righteousness.

I confess that as I become more God-inside-minded, I can more easily recognize the inward witness of the Holy Spirit. I hear the voice of the Good Shepherd, and a stranger's voice I will not follow. I am aware that my spirit is the candle of the Lord.

I meditate in the Word day and night, not letting it depart from my mouth. I test my inward witness with the Word, for the Spirit and the Word agree. I am quick to act on the Word, as well as the prompting of my spirit. I am not a hearer only, but a doer. Therefore, I am blessed in all my deeds.

Scripture References: 1 Corinthians 6:19; Philemon 6; John 16:13; Romans 8:14; Psalm 37:23; Proverbs 16:3, 3:5-6; Psalm 23:3, *The Amplified Bible;* Romans 8:16; John 10:5, 27; Proverbs 20:27; Joshua 1:8; 1 John 5:7; James 1:25.

A Prayer for Your Finances

Heavenly Father, I have chosen Jesus as the Lord of my life and I seek first Your kingdom and Your righteousness, believing that the material things I need will be supplied. I choose for my character and moral disposition to be free from the love of money, greed, lust and craving for earthly possessions. I am satisfied with my present circumstances and with what I have, being confident, because You have promised You will not in any way fail me, nor leave me without support. I am confident in Your faithfulness, that You will never leave me, nor forsake me, nor leave me helpless.

I take comfort and am encouraged. I boldly say, that the Lord is my helper and I will not be seized with alarm. I will not fear, or dread or be terrified.

I believe, Father, that You wish above all things that I prosper and be in health even as my soul prospers. I will meditate in Your Word day and night, not letting it depart from my mouth, keeping it in the midst of my heart, observing to do all that is written therein. I believe then I shall make my way prosperous and have good success. You have promised that as a doer of the Word I will be blessed in all my deeds. I am assured that You will withhold no good thing from me as I walk uprightly. The uncompromising are never forsaken. I make it my ambition to live quietly and peacefully, to mind my own affairs, to work with my hands so that I may bear myself becomingly, correctly and honorably and command the respect of the outside world, being self-supporting, dependent on no one and having need of nothing.

Knowing through Your Word, Father, that You are the Lord my God who teaches me to profit and who leads me by the way I should go, I will put Your principles to work in my life regarding employment. I choose to apply myself to good deeds—to honest labor and honorable employment—so that I may be able to meet necessary demands whenever the occasion may require, and that I may not live an idle, uncultivated, unfruitful life, in Jesus' Name.

I labor so that I may walk honestly toward those who are without. As I give, it is given to me again—good measure, pressed down, shaken together and running over—do men give into my bosom. I do not sow sparingly and grudgingly, but rather, I sow generously, blessing others. Therefore, I can expect to reap generously and with blessings.

Scripture References: Matthew 6:33; Hebrews 13:5-6, *The Amplified Bible;* 3 John 2; Joshua 1:8; Psalm 84:11; James 1:25; 1 Thessalonians 4:11-12, *The Amplified Bible;* Isaiah 48:17; Titus 3:14, *The Amplified Bible;* 1 Thessalonians 4:12; Luke 6:38; 2 Corinthians 9:6.

Overcoming Bad Habits

Father, I believe that my faith becomes effectual—divinely energized—by the acknowledging of every good thing which is in me, in Christ Jesus. Through my union with Christ, I am a new creature. Old things are passed away and all things have become new.

I was crucified with Christ, nevertheless I live, yet not I, but Christ lives in me. I was buried with Him in baptism, and raised together with Him by the power of the Holy Spirit so that I might habitually live and behave in newness of life. My old, unrenewed self was nailed to the Cross with Him in order that my body, which is the instrument of sin, might be made ineffective and inactive for evil and that I might no longer be the slave of sin.

Just as death no longer has power over Jesus Christ, neither does sin have dominion over me, through my union with Him. I consider myself dead to sin and my relation to it broken. I am alive only to God, living in unbroken fellowship with Him, in Christ Jesus.

I have been delivered from the control and dominion of darkness and transferred into the kingdom of light. I have been raised together with Christ and am seated together with Him, far above principalities, powers, rulers of the darkness of this world and wicked spirits in high places. Sin shall no longer exert dominion over me, but I have dominion over sin. It is under my feet, in the Name of Jesus, Amen.

Scripture References: Philemon 6; 2 Corinthians 5:17; Galatians 2:20; Romans 6:4, 6, 10-11, 14; Colossians 1:13, *The Amplified Bible;* Ephesians 1:21, 2:6; 6:12.

Spiritual Growth

Heavenly Father, I cease not to pray for _____, that You may grant him/her a spirit of wisdom and revelation and insight into mysteries and secrets—in the deep and intimate knowledge of You, having the eyes of his/her heart flooded with light so that he/she can know and understand the hope to which You have called him/her, and to know how rich Your glorious inheritance is in the saints.

I pray that _____ walks, lives and conducts himself/herself in a manner worthy of You, fully pleasing to You and desiring to please You in all things, bearing fruit in every good work and steadily growing and increasing in the knowledge of You. I pray that he/she may be invigorated and strengthened with all power by Your Spirit to exercise every kind of endurance and patience, perseverance and forbearance with joy.

I believe the good work You began in _____ will continue, right up to the time of Jesus' return, perfecting it and bringing it to its full completion in him/her, in Jesus' Name. Amen.

Scripture References from *The Amplified Bible:* Ephesians 1:17-19; Colossians 1:10-11; Philippians 1:6.

Conclusion

I have shared with you principles and precepts from God's Word that I have put to work in my personal life and ministry. Before Jesus came into my life, I was a total failure. Any success I have enjoyed has been the result of a personal relationship with Jesus and a rich prayer life.

Let me lead you into the throne room of God. You can enjoy the very best life has to offer and experience the success God desires for you.

Heavenly Father, I approach Your throne boldly in the Name of Jesus. I have seen from Your Word that You desire to be personally involved in my life. It is Your desire to answer my prayers. I believe that Jesus died and suffered the punishment for my sins so I could experience a close relationship with You as my heavenly Father.

I can see from Your Word that I have the right to expect my prayers to be answered—not based on my worthiness, but based on my right-standing in Christ Jesus. Your Word says if I draw near to You, You will draw near to me. I desire a more personal relationship with You and want to experience a rich and successful prayer life. I thank You for the love You have expressed toward me through Your Word. I will respond to that love right now and expect You to manifest Yourself in my life as I act on Your Word in faith. As I apply the principles I have learned, I expect to see the results of an accurate prayer life. I thank You and praise You for Your faithfulness, in Jesus' Name. Amen!

Prayer for Salvation and Baptism
in the Holy Spirit

Heavenly Father, I come to You in the Name of Jesus. Your Word says, "Whosoever shall call on the name of the Lord shall be saved" (Acts 2:21). I am calling on You. I pray and ask Jesus to come into my heart and be Lord over my life according to Romans 10:9-10: "If thou shalt confess with thy mouth the Lord Jesus, and shalt believe in thine heart that God hath raised him from the dead, thou shalt be saved. For with the heart man believeth unto righteousness; and with the mouth confession is made unto salvation." I do that now. I confess that Jesus is Lord, and I believe in my heart that God raised Him from the dead. I repent of sin. I renounce it. I renounce the devil and everything he stands for. Jesus is my Lord.

I am now reborn! I am a Christian—a child of Almighty God! I am saved! You also said in Your Word, "If ye then, being evil, know how to give good gifts unto your children: HOW MUCH MORE shall your heavenly Father give the Holy Spirit to them that ask him?" (Luke 11:13). I'm also asking You to fill me with the Holy Spirit. Holy Spirit, rise up within me as I praise God. I fully expect to speak with other tongues as You give me the utterance (Acts 2:4). In Jesus' Name. Amen!

Begin to praise God for filling you with the Holy Spirit. Speak those words and syllables you receive—not in your own language, but the language given to you by the Holy Spirit. You have to use your own voice. God will not force you to speak. Don't be concerned with how it sounds. It is a heavenly language!

Continue with the blessing God has given you and pray in the spirit every day.

You are a born-again, Spirit-filled believer. You'll never be the same!

Find a good church that boldly preaches God's Word and obeys it. Become part of a church family who will love and care for you as you love and care for them.

We need to be connected to each other. It increases our strength in God. It's God's plan for us.

Make it a habit to watch the Believer's Voice of Victory Network and become a doer of the Word, who is blessed in his doing (James 1:22-25).

About the Author

Kenneth Copeland is co-founder and president of Kenneth Copeland Ministries in Fort Worth, Texas, and best-selling author of books that include *Honor—Walking in Honesty, Truth and Integrity,* and *THE BLESSING of The LORD Makes Rich and He Adds No Sorrow With It.*

Since 1967, Kenneth has been a minister of the gospel of Christ and teacher of God's Word. He is also the artist on award-winning albums such as his Grammy-nominated *Only the Redeemed, In His Presence, He Is Jehovah, Just a Closer Walk* and *Big Band Gospel.* He also co-stars as the character Wichita Slim in the children's adventure videos *The Gunslinger, Covenant Rider* and the movie *The Treasure of Eagle Mountain,* and as Daniel Lyon in the Commander Kellie and the Superkids™ videos *Armor of Light* and *Judgment: The Trial of Commander Kellie.* Kenneth also co-stars as a Hispanic godfather in the 2009 and 2016 movies *The Rally* and *The Rally 2: Breaking the Curse.*

With the help of offices and staff in the United States, Canada, England, Australia, South Africa, Ukraine and Singapore, Kenneth is fulfilling his vision to boldly preach the uncompromised WORD of God from the top of this world, to the bottom, and all the way around. His ministry reaches millions of people worldwide through daily and Sunday TV broadcasts, magazines, teaching audios and videos, conventions and campaigns, and the World Wide Web.

Learn more about Kenneth Copeland Ministries
by visiting our website at **kcm.org**

Believer's Voice of **VICTORY**

When The LORD first spoke to Kenneth and Gloria Copeland about starting the *Believer's Voice of Victory* magazine...

He said: *This is your seed. Give it to everyone who ever responds to your ministry, and don't ever allow anyone to pay for a subscription!*

For more than 50 years, it has been the joy of Kenneth Copeland Ministries to bring the good news to believers. Readers enjoy teaching from ministers who write from lives of living contact with God, and testimonies from believers experiencing victory through God's WORD in their everyday lives.

Today, the *BVOV* magazine is mailed monthly, bringing encouragement and blessing to believers around the world. Many even use it as a ministry tool, passing it on to others who desire to know Jesus and grow in their faith!

Request your FREE subscription to the
***Believer's Voice of Victory* magazine today!**

Go to **freevictory.com** to subscribe online, or call us at
1-800-600-7395 (U.S. only) or **+1-817-852-6000**.

We're Here for You!®

Your growth in God's WORD and victory in Jesus are at the very center of our hearts. In every way God has equipped us, we will help you deal with the issues facing you, so you can be the **victorious overcomer** He has planned for you to be.

The mission of Kenneth Copeland Ministries is about all of us growing and going together. Our prayer is that you will take full advantage of all The LORD has given us to share with you.

Wherever you are in the world, you can watch the *Believer's Voice of Victory* broadcast on television (check your local listings), the Internet at kcm.org or on our digital Roku channel.

Our website, **kcm.org,** gives you access to every resource we've developed for your victory. And, you can find contact information for our international offices in Africa, Australia, Canada, Europe, Ukraine and our headquarters in the United States.

Each office is staffed with devoted men and women, ready to serve and pray with you. You can contact the worldwide office nearest you for assistance, and you can call us for prayer at our U.S. number, +1-817-852-6000, 24 hours every day!

We encourage you to connect with us often and let us be part of your everyday walk of faith!

Jesus Is LORD!

Kenneth & Gloria Copeland

Kenneth and Gloria Copeland

CPSIA information can be obtained
at www.ICGtesting.com
Printed in the USA
BVHW030408151022
649198BV00005B/6